Follow Me!

Six Lessons on How to Be a Disciple of Jesus

Dr. Tim Vanden Langenberg

Follow Me!

Copyright © 2018 Dr. Tim Vanden Langenberg

All rights reserved.

ISBN: 978-1-945975-96-7

Published by EA Books Publishing a division of Living Parables of Central Florida, Inc. a 501c3

EABooksPublishing.com

DEDICATION

I dedicate this book to my beautiful wife, JoAnn. She is my greatest encourager, my perfect helpmate, and one who sees God's possibilities in me, even when I don't see them in myself.

CONTENTS

Foreword	v
Introduction — Follow Me!	vii
Lesson 1 — Telling Others About Jesus Christ – First Why, Then How	1
Lesson 2 — Praying—The Secret to Following Christ or, How to Converse with God	14
Lesson 3 — The Importance of Reading & Studying Your Bible	28
Lesson 4 — Connecting to the Body of Christ, a Local Church	42
Lesson 5 — Following Your Pastor—Your Shepherd	57
Lesson 6 — Spirit-Led Living	70
Epilogue	88
Appendix A — Read the Bible in One Year	89
Appendix B — Who I Am in Christ	102
Appendix C — Resources	106

FOREWORD

Welcome to *Follow Me*, a discipleship Bible study designed to help you draw closer to Jesus Christ.

This study is written for new believers, newly recommitted believers, or long-time believers desiring a breakthrough in faith. It will be more effective in helping students become disciples of Jesus Christ through group study. This would fulfill the effects of Acts 2:42, which states that after the day of Pentecost, the new Christians "continued steadfastly in the apostles' doctrine and fellowship, in the breaking of bread, and in prayers."

The best way to engage this study is through one-on-one meetings, a more seasoned disciple and a newer disciple studying together. However, the more seasoned disciple should not simply expect to "teach" the new disciple how to live like Jesus. They should both grow and develop through this study. A second way this could also be done is in a small group in which participants are of various levels of commitment or discipleship in their local church(es). A third way to use this study is for pastors or other church leaders or teachers to engage in a church-wide discipleship study.

At any and all levels, the leaders, teachers, and disciplers should do the study along with those being discipled, even while explaining, teaching, and growing through the experience.

You could do this study on your own. However, the Lord will bless you most when you fellowship, study, and grow together with another Christian in conjunction with His church.

May you become everything the Lord Jesus Christ has planned for you.

Dr. Tim Vanden Langenberg
July 4, 2018

INTRODUCTION

FOLLOW ME!

In 1964 in southwestern Wisconsin, state visionaries converted an old railroad line into a biking and hiking trail and called it "The Elroy-Sparta Trail" because it ran between the two cities of Elroy and Sparta. It was the first "rails to trails" project in North America and more than 60,000 bicyclists travel the 32-plus mile trail each year, not to mention hikers, runners, and snowmobilers.

One of the charming features of the trail—or possibly eerie, depending on your perspective—is the existence of three tunnels, dating back to the early 1870's when the railroad was built. The longest of these tunnels is nearly three quarters of a mile long.

What makes it eerie to some travelers is the darkness inside the tunnels. That's right! There are no lights in the tunnels. So, hikers and bikers need to bring flashlights with them in order to avoid stepping into the drainage trenches at the base of the walls and falling into the walls themselves. The darkness inside is so dense that travelers cannot see from one end of the tunnel to the other.

Standing at the entrance of that tunnel and peering in can make some people nervous. The sound of water dripping inside can be heard at the archway (pictured above), which makes some wonder if it is safe. Inside the tunnel within a few feet of that archway, the temperature drops to subterranean levels. Even on the hottest summer days, a jacket is recommended inside.

Groups of bikers—and often families with children—will stop to take a break before entering. They get out their flashlights, put on their jackets or sweatshirts, and take a drink to prepare themselves for the three-quarter mile walk. Then the person designated as the leader usually says something like, "Follow me!" and off the leader heads into the tunnel, followed by the rest of the group, to disappear into the darkness.

Jesus Christ of Nazareth said those same words to many people throughout His earthly ministry, "Follow Me." It was a call for the people who heard it to go beyond the role of curiosity seeker, entertainment chaser, or spiritual adventure hunter. Jesus gave a name to the people who followed Him and lived by His words. He called them disciples. They became disciplined students who found themselves changed by the Son of God. As a result of their transformation—what Jesus called being born again, these disciples lived life, saw the world, and understood eternity differently than they did before they met Jesus.

Their lives—their destinies—have been eternally changed by the Son of God whose name is "Immanuel, which is translated 'God with us'" (Matthew 1:23).[1] But, the

Bible says that "Jesus Christ is the same yesterday, today, and forever" (Hebrews 13:8). That means Jesus is the same Son of God today as He was 2000 years ago. He still changes people's lives and their destinies.

Now it is your turn to encounter Jesus Christ of Nazareth, to hear His teachings, to let His commands and His heavenly perspective challenge your worldly beliefs, to see Him crucified for your sins, and raised to life for your salvation. It is your turn to encounter Jesus and to intentionally respond to His call, "Follow Me!"

In these pages lies a pattern of discipline as a disciple of Jesus Christ. It is a way for each believer to become more like Jesus—to study His ways, His words, His attitudes, and His unique position as both God and human. If you will study Jesus and let Him lead you, you will find power for living this life and fearless hope as you face life in the next.

May your journey with Jesus Christ—as His disciple—be filled with joy, hope, love, and victory according to His Word.

---

[1] All Scripture quotations, unless otherwise noted, are from the New King James Version (NKJV).

LESSON 1

TELLING OTHERS ABOUT JESUS CHRIST FIRST WHY, THEN HOW

One Saturday morning, a salesman stopped by the office of the company at which he was employed. One of his coworkers was there catching up on some work.

After exchanging greetings and a bit of chit-chat, the coworker talked virtually nonstop for almost forty-five minutes, explaining the reasons he didn't practice the religion of his parents (who were Jewish), why he considered organized religion to be unnecessary, why being a good person is enough in life, and why Christians should not push their religion on the rest of the world. His mild rant would be better described as a monologue because he alone did all the talking.

Suddenly, he said he did not want to continue the conversation and that he didn't like feeling pressured into engaging in religious discussions. The salesman responded, "All I said was that I was surprised anyone was here on a Saturday." His coworker said he thought he was being questioned as to why he was not in synagogue that morning. The salesman did not even know he was Jewish and afterward admitted that it was a weird conversation.

Many people have had those kinds of verbal interactions. In fact, you may have been on one end or the other of that dialogue at some point.

If you don't know *why* you would talk to another person about Jesus Christ, then you do not need to learn *how* to talk with someone about the Lord. If the motivation—the *why*—is not there, the resulting action—the *how*—will not follow.

If you look at the people who encountered Jesus in the gospels, they did not have any trouble talking about Jesus. Look up these verses and see why people talked so much about Jesus.

- Mark 1:21-39 – Why was everyone looking for Jesus? Was it not because He miraculously healed sick people and cast out demons?
- John 6:1-35 – Why did the crowds of people chase after Jesus, running around the lake (Sea of Galilee) and then rowing back across? Was it for the free food?
- John 11:45-57 – Why did the religious leaders talk about Jesus so much? Were they so jealous of Him that they began to plot His murder?
- Matthew 16:13-20 – Why did the disciples talk about Jesus? What did Peter say they believed to be true about Jesus of Nazareth?

What about you? What do you think about Jesus? What do you say about Him, if you say anything at all? Do you believe that Jesus is "the Christ, the Son of the living God?"

Read Romans 10:9. Do you believe—meaning you put all your faith, hope, and trust—in Jesus Christ as Lord? Do you believe that He is risen from the dead? If you have not believed up until now, stop and settle this before you move on. Confess your sins, repent—that means turn away from your sins—and declare out loud that Jesus Christ is your Lord. If you believe that Jesus is Lord and that God raised Him from the dead, you are a Christian, a new creation of God in Christ. You are spiritually reborn!

THE NEW YOU

You may or may not feel different right at this moment. But God does not lie in His Word. God clearly said in 2 Corinthians 5:17, "Therefore, if anyone is in Christ, he is a new creation." God has made you into a new creation: His very own son or daughter. Your sins are now forgiven. You are reconciled to God, in right standing with Him. Jesus now lives in you by faith. Your eternity is secured in Him. You are no longer a slave to sin, bound to the kingdom of darkness, but you have been conveyed to the kingdom of the light of God's Son. You are highly favored and loved by God, have been seated in heavenly places, and have your name written on God's honor roll called the Lamb's Book of Life. All these things are now true about you according to God's Word (John 1:12, 1 John 1:9, 2 Corinthians 5:17-19,

Galatians 2:20, Romans 8:1-11, John 8:31-36, John 3:16, Ephesians 2:4-10, Revelation 21:22-27).

Your mind may have a difficult time accepting the truth about your new self. The devil will try to tell you it isn't true. But God knows what is true more than any other being. So, if the Lord God says that these things are true about you, then these things are true. Therefore, begin telling yourself—your mind, your emotions/feelings, and your body—to accept these truths.

As you begin to grasp the truth about what Jesus Christ has done for you, you will also begin to realize just how great, awesome, and wonderful Jesus is. And you will want to share how magnificent and astonishing He is with others.

Now you have the why—the motivation—for telling others about Jesus Christ.

PASS IT ON

Today, tell someone what God has done for you. Tell your story, or at least a small part of it, to relate to another human being that Jesus Christ still works in people's lives. Your sheer enthusiasm will be of interest to other people.

But, you will soon find that not everyone wants to listen to you. Not everyone is happy to hear about Jesus. Not everyone believes he or she needs a Savior. In fact, you may soon find some rather stiff resistance to hearing your testimony. When that happens, don't fret. As you read through the gospels and the book of The Acts of the Apostles (usually called Acts) you will find that Jesus and the apostles often encountered significant opposition when they spoke.

You may encounter moments of self-doubt and times of fear to share your faith. Society today is filled with people who say it's OK to believe whatever you want as long as you don't share it with anyone. Both the government and the media are increasingly intolerant of biblical Christianity. These two entities work hard to shape the attitudes and beliefs of society.

That is exactly what the apostles faced in their day in the Roman Empire, from "Jerusalem, and in all Judea and Samaria, and to the end of the earth" (Acts 1:8). Remember, God uses believers like you to spread the good news of Jesus Christ in the face of opposition in order to show that He is Lord. History has proven that the stronger the opposition, the more people need the gospel.

Why do Christians get so stressed out about sharing their faith with other people? In the last few years there have been some high profile instances of Christians "witnessing" by shouting at passers-by, calling them names, and telling them they are bound for hell. Many people—including many Christians—find this type of witnessing offensive. These public demonstrations have been held at funerals of military personnel and political figures, which makes it all the more distressing to the people of those communities and even to the rest of the country.

Many Christians in churches and communities take great offense to this type of witnessing. They may wonder if that type of witnessing produces any positive effect. One perspective allows that answer to be Yes!

Because such harsh declarations of judgment offend so many, people who normally would not ask questions about Christ want to know if that is real Christianity. So, they talk to Christians they know through work, school, or activities—people they know and generally trust. These Christians then have the opportunity to share their faith in Christ following a public display of harsh street preaching and Christian protests.

Perhaps the real question about the street preachers is whether they—those who are offended—are actually alright with God. Their questions may be motivated by fear—fear of judgment, fear of hell, fear of damnation, and even fear of God. They may not know for certain where they stand when it comes to spiritual things.

Jesus Christ calls every Christian to be a witness on His behalf. Christians are commissioned, like officers in the military, to carry out the mission of Jesus Christ. Old hymns like *Onward Christian Soldiers* and *Marching to Zion* convey the image of the church as the army of the Lord.

Perhaps the church could also be compared to a great symphony orchestra. Jesus Christ is the composer. The pastor of the church is the conductor and Christians are the musicians—and at the same time, the musical instruments they play. Our lives play the music composed by Christ. But each musician [Christian] can't go off, playing his or her own tune. The entire orchestra plays what Christ composed. The Church follows the Great Commission of Jesus Christ.

All four gospels include words by Jesus Christ, which He spoke in the forty days between His resurrection and ascension. These words are commands and a commissioning to His disciples to share the gospel. Read these following verses.

- Matthew 28:19-20
- Mark 16:15
- Luke 24:46-48
- John 20:21

Witnessing is the act of a human believer—a Christian—opening the door for the Holy Spirit to work in the life of a person who does not yet believe. The Holy Spirit gives Christians the words to speak, then uses those words to bring about the spiritual rebirth of the hearer. That is the job of the Holy Spirit. The witness simply delivers the message. So, just deliver God's message using God's Word. You don't have to be clever or know everything there is to know. All you have to do is tell another person what you know—that Jesus Christ saved you from your sins.

Some Christian witnesses may feel self-conscious about what they should say. Some experience a sensation of uneasiness, fearing they may say the wrong thing. But, don't worry. God has an entire book full of words to say at the right time. That is a key reason for you to learn parts of the Bible. When you read a verse, you can then remember it. When you remember it, you can repeat it to someone else. When someone else hears it, God is able to work in that person through His words.

Look up Romans 10:17. This verse says that God gives faith through the sharing of His Word.

Here is one more thought. Acts 1:8 states that believers will receive power when they are baptized in the Holy Spirit. Then they will *be* witnesses for Jesus, not simply witness about Jesus. That means that everything about their lives will display how great His transforming and regenerating power is. Their words, actions, mannerisms, lifestyle, purchasing choices, in other words, everything about them will demonstrate the power of Jesus Christ to save, heal, and deliver.

If you have not been baptized in the Holy Spirit, seek this great gift now. Ask your mentor or pastor. You need the Holy Spirit to live in these last days of history.

STUDY TIME

Memorize as many of these Scriptures as you can this week. Read them. Write them on cards or slips of paper. Put them up on your bathroom mirror, refrigerator, bulletin board, on your phone, or carry them in your purse or wallet so you can read them multiple times throughout the day. Say them to yourself over and over again until they become part of your memory. Remind yourself that they apply to you and to every other person you meet.

- John 3:16
- Romans 3:23
- Romans 6:23
- Romans 10:9
- Acts 3:19

If you find yourself having trouble remembering all five, then memorize one – or perhaps two. Pick your favorite and memorize it. But, write out all five and read them all every day.

In order to share with other people, you will need to be able to find these five verses in your Bible. Perhaps you will want to put a marker at each page so you can easily access them. You may also wish to underline or accent each verse, for example, using highlight markers.

To help you in reciting these verses, ask your mentor, the person who gave you this book, or a trusted Christian friend from church to sit down and listen to you open your Bible to each verse and recite it or read it. This will help you become comfortable with sharing these verses.

Next, ask a non-Christian friend to listen to you read and recite the verses. This person should be someone who will listen sympathetically without ridiculing you for your new faith in Jesus.

TELLING YOUR STORY

Most people think there is nothing special about their own lives. But you have a unique story and God can use it to communicate His love to other people. When you tell about how Jesus Christ intervened in your life and made you a new creation, those hearing it will be encouraged to know God still works in real people's lives.

A good way to tell your story is using a pattern found in a book entitled *Becoming a Contagious Christian* by Bill Hybels and Mark Mittelberg (Grand Rapids, MI: Zondervan, 1994). The pattern has three parts: BC (Before Christ), the Cross (when Christ intervened), and AD (how you and your life are different since Christ came in).

Telling your story of how you believed in Jesus or how Jesus helped you in your time of need should be short, sweet, and to the point. Make it no more than two minutes long. Don't be one of those people who talks for an hour and a half, telling his or her entire life story, complete with recounting details of every ache and pain. (Frankly, that bores the listener.) So, keep it short and keep the focus on Jesus Christ.

You could even diagram this out on a sheet of paper.

BC	✝	AD

The three parts should proceed like this:

1. BC – Relate briefly about what you or your circumstances were like before you came to faith in Christ. What major issues or problems did you face? You don't need to give gory details. People will get the idea.
2. The Cross – Share how Jesus came to you by faith. How did the critical event of faith happen in that moment? What were you thinking or feeling at that time? Did God speak a word to you? Tell what

happened when you believed in, turned to, or cried out to Jesus for help.
3. AD – Tell what life is like since you trusted in Jesus. How is Jesus faithfully leading, feeding, and guarding you in life, especially in relation to the previous problem mentioned? This is your opportunity to tell about how great your God is.
4. The Follow-up – Ask the listener for a response. Has she or he ever encountered a similar situation and needed help? Does he or she believe in Jesus? Would she or he be willing to pray for help and/or salvation right now?

Remember to keep the whole story under two minutes. Use God's Word whenever possible and focus on Jesus Christ.

A NEW PATH

You have now begun a journey on a new path: the path of discipleship. It is as if you are one of the disciples on the road with Jesus of Nazareth. You are filled with joy and expectation because the Son of God is leading you and speaking directly to you.

Close your study by reading Psalm 23 and thanking Jesus that He is your Good Shepherd.

SCRIPTURES TO STUDY

Jesus at work

- Mark 1:21-39

- John 6:1-35
- John 11:45-57 (Read all of Chapter 11 for the story of the raising of Lazarus from the dead)
- Matthew 16:13-20

The truth about Jesus and the truth about you

- Romans 10:9
- What is God saying to you right now?

_____

_____

- 2 Corinthians 5:17-19, John 1:12, 1 John 1:9, Galatians 2:19-20, Romans 8:1-11, John 8:31-36, Ephesians 2:4-10, Revelation 21:22-27
- How does it feel to have God say this about you?

_____

_____

Telling the story – Being a witness

- Acts 1:8
- Matthew 28:19-20, Mark 16:15-18, Luke 24:46-48, John 20:21 – You are commissioned by Jesus Himself
- John 3:16
- Romans 3:23, 6:23, 10:9 – these verses are often called "The Roman Road"
- Acts 3:19

- Psalm 23

Do you sense a change in you because the Word of God is in your heart and mind?

_____

_____

LESSON 2

PRAYING – THE SECRET TO FOLLOWING CHRIST OR, HOW TO CONVERSE WITH GOD

The following sign was posted in a college library.

> **ABSOLUTELY NO TALKING**
> Other students are studying
> If there is disruptive conversation, send an email to:
> *[email address@the college]* Library Technician

Apparently, students carried on verbal conversations with one another so loudly that it disrupted the communication of other students with their study materials, that is, with their books, notes, etc. To remedy this violation of the library's rules, the offended student(s) should not speak to the offending students face-to-face, nor should they speak with library staff face-to-face. They should send an electronic message (email) to the Library Technician.

The design of the sign, with its progressively smaller font size, also sent a clear message. That message was two-fold. First, the library administration does not allow talking in that area of the library. Second, should someone violate this rule, the library administration hopes no one reports it so that the administrators do not have to deal with it. In short, all communication—except for quiet reading—is discouraged.

Instances like this show that we are training ourselves not to communicate with others—at least, not to communicate well.

But that is not God's intention for us. God wants to speak with us and wants us to speak with Him. He wants conversation that strengthens our relationship with Him. That conversation is called prayer.

... TIME ...

Stories abound in the history of the church about great saints of old who spent hours each day and weeks and months each year in prayer. Pastors and teachers repeat the stories of how those saints rose in the wee hours of the morning and stayed up until the late hours of the night to pray. For centuries church leaders held up these practices as the holiest of the holy ones.

Stories like these can serve to condemn Christians for not praying more and spending more time with God. But, God does not compare you with people who lived hundreds of years ago. Your relationship with your spouse or children should not be judged on marriages and families from the Middle Ages in Europe. So, don't let anyone put that kind of guilt on you and your love relationship with the Lord.

God simply wants to talk with you.

The book of Psalms in the Old Testament is one of the most beautiful books in the Bible because it gives a voice to every person in the world, regardless of importance. These Psalms also reveal to us the many situations faced by the people who wrote them, how they brought their life situations to God, and how the Lord responded. For example, King David penned several Psalms when he was on the run for his life. Sometimes every second counted in his escape. But he always found time to praise God and to call out for help from His Savior, the Lord Jehovah.

Two things emerge when we look at how godly people prayed in the Bible. 1) They took time to be alone on a daily basis so they could talk with God. 2) They stayed in constant communication with the Lord as they went through their days.

As a new and/or growing Christian, look at how you spend your time. You may think you do not have time to pray and talk with God. But, if you examine your schedule—even the time you sleep—you may learn something about yourself. You may find time spent in activities that do not honor God, for example, long hours watching television or movies (especially those that glorify sex, violence, and other unholy attitudes). Or you may spend vast amounts of time on your phone or on the internet. Maybe you are wasting your life stopping in at bars, taverns, or clubs. (At the end of the week, your paycheck is gone, your head and body are sick, and your friends are in as bad of shape as you.) What will you tell Jesus about how you spent the life He gave you?

TIME IN THE WORD

You have priorities in your life and those priorities changed when you believed in Jesus Christ as Lord. Think about the things you consider most important in life. This question is not, "What do you want to be when you grow up?" But do take an honest assessment of what you consider most important in your day-to-day activities. Have those activities taken you where you would like to go? Have they taken you where the Lord wants you to go?

Read the following passages and think about what they mean in relation to your priorities, God's priorities, and how you spend your time.

- Joshua 1:1-9

o What command does God give Joshua three separate times in these verses?

_____

_____

_____

- How do these commands apply to you and your day-to-day life?

  _____
  _____
  _____

- How does v. 8 apply to you today? And how can you follow what God tells Joshua in this verse?

  _____
  _____
  _____

* Psalm 119 (the whole Psalm, but especially vs. 89-112)

  - God's word is "forever settled in heaven," so why should we ever doubt it here on earth? Are there times when you find it hard to believe or apply God's word to your life? What could you do to remedy this?

    _____
    _____

- Following God's word keeps us from sin, delivers us out of evil and directs our steps toward good. Have you seen this work in your life? How?

  _____

  _____

  _____

- What successes has God given you in life? This week? Today?

  _____

  _____

- Romans 12:1-2

- "A living sacrifice" – What might you need to sacrifice to become more like Jesus?

  _____

  _____

  _____

- "Be transformed by the renewing of your mind" – What attitudes and thought patterns in your mind are ungodly, un-Christlike, or not conformed to the Word of God?

ALONE TIME IN THE WORD WITH GOD

As people age, they often notice that, in a crowded room where music is playing or members of the crowd are talking, they may have a hard time hearing and understanding what someone says to them in a conversation. All the ambient sounds—the background noise—drowns out the one person they want to hear.

The same is true in your life with God. There are so many distractions that may keep you from hearing God's voice: phones, tablets, computers, TVs, sports, work, friends, music, social media, advertising, shopping, food and dining, hanging out, even family. If you want to hear the voice of the Lord, you must make the effort to turn off everything else and listen for it.

In John 10:3-4 & 27, Jesus made this astounding promise. "The sheep hear his [the shepherd's] voice; and he calls his own sheep by name and leads them out. And when he brings out his own sheep, he goes before them; and the sheep follow him, for they know his voice. ... My sheep hear My voice, and I know them, and they follow Me."

Jesus' promise means several things for you. 1) Jesus talks to you. He speaks through His Word, the Bible. He speaks through your pastor and other Christians. He speaks directly into your own spirit. Make no mistake, Jesus talks to you! 2) You can hear His voice. It will take a bit of training to develop voice recognition. This means you need to disconnect from other "voices" and sounds just to listen for it. Listening is hard work at first and it requires intentional focus to hear the right voice. 3) Once you hear the voice of Jesus, your best response is to follow. There is a word that rightly describes your choice and action of following: obedience. Sheep follow the shepherd because it is in their best interest to do so. The shepherd leads the sheep to pasture and water and protects them from predators and thieves.

Read Psalm 23 to see what a great shepherd Jesus Christ is for His sheep. Can you look back over your life and see times when Jesus provided for you, protected you, and led you—even when you weren't expecting it?

_____

_____

WHY PRAY?

Humans who have been born again, that is, spiritually reborn by the Holy Spirit through faith in Jesus Christ, have a great privilege and a powerful secret in facing life on earth. It's called prayer. Christians can simply call this effective power known as prayer by one word: relationship.

Prayer is developing a growing, healthy relationship with the Almighty God through Jesus Christ by the power of the Holy Spirit. As you draw closer to His presence, you leave behind the weight that holds you down in this world. You begin to see things from a heavenly perspective. You value the things that your Father God values. You begin to love the things that Jesus loves. You say and do the things that the Holy Spirit prompts in you. His voice becomes clearer. His Word becomes more understandable. His will becomes more recognizable.

In prayer, your faith in Jesus Christ grows, develops, exercises, and strengthens. Pray to tap into His great power. Pray to draw life from His fountain of living water. Pray to become more like Him.

Even so, many people think prayer is simply presenting to God their grocery list of wants. They never grow beyond the prayers they learned as a five or six-year-old. "Bless mommy and daddy and grandma and grandpa and brother and sister. Bless my dog, Fido, and my fish, Bubbles. And please help me to have fun at recess tomorrow." That may be fine when you are a child, but it's not the kind of prayer the Bible presents for spiritually strong adults.

Read James 5:13-18. What kind of impact does prayer have on life in this world? These verses mention suffering, sickness, forgiveness, even the weather. So ... how should you pray?

HOW TO PRAY

There are two basic times to pray in the day. One is during a designated, set-aside time where you talk and listen to God, read and meditate upon His Word. The other is the rest of the day in which you keep constant conversations with God going. You can pray in your car, at work, in the restroom, walking down the hall, in a store, in between meetings, at meals, etc. Sometimes you can spend the day meditating on something you heard from God or His Word when you spoke with Him earlier. Or perhaps something occurs during the day and you pray over it or about it at the time and/or for the next few hours.

Many Christians can give testimonies of witnessing car accidents (or other kinds of tragedies) in which they immediately prayed over the victims for life, healing, comfort, and peace, even as paramedics and police were on the way. They may not have known it at the time, but, because they were already in communication with the Lord, they were able to hold up the ones in desperate need of help in a moment's notice.

So, *how* do we actually pray?

Posture can be important. Sometimes you may feel the need to walk as you pray. Sometimes you may need to kneel or bow yourself down before God. You may wish to sit so you can read the Bible more easily. Bowing your head and folding your hands may help occasionally. Raising your hands may be needed at times. When tragedy strikes, for example, families and friends huddle together, holding one another with their heads down, weeping in sorrow. When people get married, they hold their heads up, clasp hands, and smile with joy at the wedding ceremony.

Read 1 Kings 8:22 & 54. How did King Solomon position himself when he prayed? People posture themselves differently for different situations. Pray in any and all situations knowing God hears you when you pray. Furthermore, if you listen carefully, you will hear His voice as well.

Read 1 John 5:14-15. Then read James 4:1-10.

- What do these verses say about prayer, about the heart and intent of the one who prays, and about God who hears the prayers?

_____

_____

_____

When you talk to God, converse naturally with Him. But, don't be too casual, flippant, or familiar. Remember He is your heavenly Father, not just some guy you met on the street. On the other hand, thou dost not need to speaketh in olde English. Bare your heart to God. Speak honestly and in your own voice.

Read Matthew 6:9-13. This is the passage we call "The Lord's Prayer." In it, Jesus teaches us to honor and praise God. But, He also teaches us to speak to God about our real lives, down to the bread we eat and the people we have trouble forgiving. This is a real-life, nitty-gritty prayer, one that makes us authentically honest with God. Take off your mask when you pray and be real with God your Father.

PRAYING IN THE SPIRIT

Jude 20-21 says, "But you, beloved, building yourselves up on your most holy faith, praying in the Holy Spirit, keep yourselves in the love of God, looking for the mercy of our Lord Jesus Christ unto eternal life." The way to build yourself up and to keep on track is to pray in the Holy Spirit.

Spirit-filled Christians will often pray in the Holy Spirit by speaking in their prayer language, one that Paul calls "tongues … of angels" (1 Cor. 13:1). That means you let the Holy Spirit pray through you using the language that He gave you at your Holy Spirit baptism.

You may not always know how to pray appropriately or what to pray for properly. When you pray in the Spirit, the Holy Spirit speaks through you, according to Romans 8:26-27. This may feel strange at first because human beings often want to be in control. But when you humble yourself before the Almighty God and pray quietly or out loud with a heavenly language, your spirit connects directly with God's Spirit and your prayer connects directly with the heart of God. The Holy Spirit then intercedes for you, lining up your prayer perfectly with God's will, always seeking the right thing.

The church also has instructions for praying in tongues together in 1 Corinthians 14:14-16. There are times when this is appropriate. Yes, it can get noisy. But even in the sounds of unknown languages, God is hearing those prayers because it is His Spirit who is interceding or speaking on behalf of those Christians. However, if you expect other people to say "Amen" to your prayers, to agree with you in accordance with God's will, then you need to speak in a known language. For most people that means their mother tongue—their original language.

Praying in tongues is at the discretion and control of the Spirit-filled Christian (1 Cor. 14:32). You can choose to pray in tongues or to pray in your everyday language. When you pray in tongues, it doesn't have to be loud. Some people pray as if they think God is deaf. They shout and scream with so much volume that they disrupt all other activity in the vicinity.

When a Spirit-filled Christian prays in the spirit, a divine connection occurs. This opens your heart to the will of God and builds you up and strengthens you in your spirit so that you can face life without fear.

Read Ephesians 6:10-20, focusing especially on v. 19.

- Notice that all the pieces of armor are defensive, in order to protect the Christian. Only the Word of God—the sword of the Spirit—is a weapon to be used on offense. And it is to be used in conjunction with prayer in the Spirit. What might that mean about how you should pray – or how you should use prayer combined with the Word?

_____

_____

_____

- What is the difference between praying and watching? (See also Matt. 26:36-46.)

_____

_____

_____

This week read a Psalm (of your choice) every day (the same Psalm) and pray it as if it were your own prayer.

LESSON 3

THE IMPORTANCE OF READING & STUDYING YOUR BIBLE

When recruits enter the U.S. Marine Corps, they go through basic training. One of the things Marines in the infantry learn is how to care for their rifles. They have a saying that begins, "This is my rifle. There are many like it. This one is mine. ..."

The one offensive weapon that Christians possess for use against their enemy, the devil, is "the sword of the Spirit, which is the word of God" (Eph. 6:17-18). It is to be wielded in prayer in the Spirit so that the word of God "shall not return to Me void, but it shall accomplish what I please, and it shall prosper in the thing for which I sent it" (Isaiah 55:11).

Even Jesus Christ the Son of God, who is called the Word of God (John 1:1), uses His word against His enemies. He demonstrated how to use the sword of the Spirit during the days of His earthly temptation (recorded in Matthew 4:1-11 and Luke 4:1-13). Revelation 19:11-16 indicates how He will use it at the close of this world's history. The fact that the Lord Jesus uses the word in such a way should convey how powerful and effective the Bible is for use in life and ministry today.

You could use lines similar to the Marine Corps teaching as you train yourself to use your Bible for everyday life.

> *This is my Bible.*
> *There are many like it.*
> *But, this is my Bible.*
> *I will discipline myself to read it and study it daily.*
> *I will learn to use it according to God's will and plan.*
> *Through it I will meet the living Word of God, Jesus Christ.*
> *And by His divine power,*
> *He gives me all things that pertain to life and godliness.*
> *By Him I receive and take possession of*
> *Every promise and blessing that God has for me.*
> *And by using it in faith I will be more than a conqueror.*
> *This is my Bible.*
> *And my God speaks to me through it. Amen!*

Perhaps you should say this as you prepare to read the Bible, as both a prayer and a declaration for spiritual battle.

That sounds rather intense, doesn't it? You may feel a strong sense of excitement to start reading your Bible and to find all those promises God made to you. But there will come a day—and that day may come much sooner than you would like—when the "shine" will be off your Christian walk and you will feel more like watching TV, playing video games, or hanging out with friends than reading your Bible.

You may find yourself thinking thoughts like, "I just don't seem to have time to read my Bible today," or "I'm so busy with life—work, family, and friends. There's no time for anything else." When you begin to think you do not have enough time to read and study your Bible, remember that you have twenty-four hours in a day just like everyone else.

Consider these: Did you take time to eat a worm today? Or did you visit the Kremlin today? Or did you go to your local hardware store and do a pirouette while wearing a pink tutu? Then ask yourself *why* you did not do any of these or any number of other odd things? The answer is that these off-beat activities are not high on your list of priorities, if they are on your list at all.

We make time to do the things we value. Conversely, we do not make time for the things we do not value.

So, ask yourself whether the things that take up every waking moment of the day are as dear to you as reading, studying, learning, and applying the Word of God to your life? Do those other activities provide the same temporal and eternal value (that means this life and the next) as God's Word?

When you examine yourself like this, you might even discover that some of your activities tend to pull you away from Jesus Christ. They may negatively influence you toward anger, violence, hatred, unfair judgment and treatment of people, unhealthy alcohol or drug use, etc. Curbing these activities and replacing them with Bible reading and study will ultimately benefit you in many ways in the long run.

The real issue is that you are now a disciple of Jesus Christ. That means His priorities became your priorities. You adopted the value system of your Lord and Master Jesus Christ because He put His holiness in you. As a result, you have lost your appetite for some of the old things you used to love.

Now if you don't "keep yourselves in the love of God, looking for the mercy of our Lord Jesus Christ unto eternal life" by "building yourselves up on your most holy faith, praying in the Holy Spirit" (Jude 20-21), you run the risk of falling back into your old ways and being more miserable because you once tasted freedom from sin.

So, get started in the Word of God. Read something every day. At the back of this book in Appendix A you will find a schedule to read the Bible through in a year. Reading the entire Bible is a good practice to get into so that you understand what it truly contains. If the sheer size of the Bible intimidates you, don't worry. You only read one word, one sentence, one paragraph, and one chapter at a time. Just enjoy the stories and learn everything you can from the Holy Spirit.

As you read, feel free to highlight or underline verses or words that make an impact as you read. This will help you find them more easily when you need them. You may want to keep a journal or notebook for notes as you read. The Holy Spirit will speak to you as read His Word. When He does, write down those thoughts and words in your notebook so that you can recall God's words to you.

Also write down verses that seem to apply to your life and spend time memorizing them. Memorization of Bible verses is important as they will then pop up in your mind at most needed times. Psalm 119:11 says, "Your word I have hidden in my heart, that I might not sin against You."

Remember you are not only reading the Bible, you are strategically studying the Word of God. Every time you read, expect to get something from the Holy Spirit. Envision yourself as one of those early disciples with Jesus on the shore, in the boat, or in the synagogue, holding on to every word your Master utters.

THE BIBLE – GOD'S STORY

The Bible is God's story from beginning to end. Yet, there are several major divisions in that story. The Bible is divided into sixty-six books. These books are divided into two major sections: the Old Testament (containing thirty-nine books) and the New Testament (containing twenty-seven books).

Testament is a word that we use in a legal sense, as in last will and testament. It is a binding word that holds people accountable to carry out the wishes of the person who wrote it. So it is with the Bible. God authored it by inspiring people to write what He said so that every person for the rest of human history could read it or hear it spoken. When God's word is read or heard, the Holy Spirit does His work in the reader's or hearer's heart. He may convict of sin, give faith, bring about a new spiritual birth (called regeneration), or illuminate God's will for today. All of these are the work of the Holy Spirit according to the word of God.

The Old Testament contains the Scriptures or sacred writings written before the birth of Jesus Christ of Nazareth. These were written down beginning about 1500 B.C. and ending about 400 B.C. (This abbreviation stands for *Before Christ*.) Many people had a hand in writing down these Scriptures. For example, the prophet Jeremiah commanded a scribe name Baruch, who worked with him, to write down some of the prophecies which the Lord God spoke to Jeremiah (see Jeremiah 36:4). The Old Testament Scriptures tell us about everything from the creation of the world to the prophecies about the coming Messiah Jesus. They include songs, poetry, history, short sayings of wisdom, and dire warnings for the future. God left nothing to chance. He increasingly revealed more and more knowledge of Himself to the world in an effort to get His children to turn toward Him and to follow Him.

The New Testament includes the Scriptures written after the birth, death, resurrection, and ascension of Jesus Christ and the sending of His Holy Spirit on the day of Pentecost. Most of the New Testament is made up of short books called epistles. These are letters written by the first generation of those who lived with and followed Jesus (called apostles) to the first churches concerning doctrines and practices that Christians must know to live everyday life while preparing for eternal life. There are also many prophecies scattered throughout the New Testament concerning the return of Jesus Christ and the events of the last days.

The apostles either directly wrote the New Testament books or gave their testimony to their followers who did the writing of those books. For example, Luke was a disciple who traveled and ministered with Paul. Luke wrote the gospel of Luke and the Acts of the Apostles (generally referred to as Acts). These books came into existence during the lives of the apostles of Jesus Christ from about the mid-40s to the mid-90s A.D. (This abbreviation stands for Anno Domini, which is Latin for *In the Year of Our Lord*. Many people think it means *After Death*.)

(Some people have begun to use the designations BCE and CE, which mean *Before the Common Era* and *Common Era* instead of B.C. and A.D. They do this, they say, out of respect for people of other faiths and cultures. But Christians understand that time itself is measured by the God who created it. Therefore, I continue to use B.C. and A.D. out of respect and honor for our Lord Jesus Christ. I mean no disrespect to other people and their religions. However, I respect and honor Jesus Christ as Lord much, much more.)

There are several powerful testimonies that God gives about His Word. Read the following and see what God says.

- Isaiah 55:6-11
- John 6:39 & 17:17
- Romans 10:17

- 2 Timothy 2:15 & 3:16-4:5
- Hebrews 1:1-4
- 2 Peter 1:16-21

What did God say to you about His Word through these verses?

_____

_____

_____

_____

HOW TO READ THE BIBLE

As mentioned above, Appendix A is a plan to read the Bible through in one calendar year. But, here is an alternative, systematic approach to read the entire New Testament. You may simply wish to start reading at Matthew and go all the way through Revelation. That is one good approach. Here is another approach. This may help you get a better grasp of New Testament teachings and doctrines.

1. Mark
2. John
3. 1 John
4. 2 John
5. 3 John
6. Matthew

7. Luke
8. Acts
9. Ephesians
10. Galatians
11. Romans
12. 1 Corinthians
13. 2 Corinthians
14. Hebrews
15. Philippians
16. Colossians
17. 1 Timothy
18. 2 Timothy
19. Titus
20. Philemon
21. James
22. 1 Peter
23. 2 Peter
24. Jude
25. 1 Thessalonians
26. 2 Thessalonians
27. Revelation

As you start reading the Bible this week, read for at least 10-15 minutes each morning or at the beginning of your day. Immediately upon the conclusion of your reading, ask God what He wants to say to you through His Word. Then be quiet and listen. Jesus Christ will speak with you (John 14:27). Ask:

- Lord, what do you have to say to me through Your Word?

- How does what You say in Your Word apply to my life circumstances?
- Is there something I need to correct or change to come into line with Your Word, Lord?
- Jesus, I know I am accepted and loved by You (Romans 5:1-2 & 8:1-2, 31-39). Am I a disciplined disciple in Your kingdom?
- What am I doing well?

You may encounter passages or verses that you have trouble understanding or that challenge your sensitivities. Do not stop reading! Ask someone for help—your pastor, a trusted leader in the church, or the person who is mentoring you through this study. Remember that you are learning to see things from God's perspective. You need to be willing to identify your own preferences and prejudices and be willing to set those aside—unlearn them if need be—in order to value what God values and to accept as truth those things God declares to be true.

While you are being so teachable in your mind and heart, make changes in your actions and habits to bring your lifestyle into line with God's Word. Be patient with yourself. Don't get frustrated if it takes time. But don't make excuses for laziness or half-hearted effort. Give the Lord Jesus Christ your very best. You will be amazed how His power will flow to enable you to succeed at your efforts to live out His Word.

One of the ways which you can immediately put God's Word to use is by your words. As you memorize even short phrases of Scripture, begin to use them in your speech as often as possible. Stop saying things that contradict God's Word and start speaking what God has already written as truth.

One Christian testified that when he was first born again, he frequently said a phrase that he was not even aware was coming out of his mouth. His all-too-often repeated phrase was, "I don't know." One day his pastor told him rather sharply to stop saying that phrase. The reason for this admonition was that he did indeed know, that he knew better, and that he knew the will of God, all because he was studying the Word of God. But, his pastor told him, because he kept repeating that phrase he was defeating himself and not letting God's Word do its work in his mind, heart, and life.

Put God's Word into your mind and heart and speak it out in your words. If you need help with declaring the truth of God's Word in your life, see Appendix B at the back of this book. These Bible affirmations speak God's truth about who and what you are in His kingdom, His church, and in your life. Read, memorize, and accept them as your new reality in Christ Jesus!

Read on, Brother! Read on, Sister!

THIS WEEK'S LOG OF BIBLE READINGS

Sunday

_____

What God said to me:

_____

_____

Monday

_____

What God said to me:

_____

_____

_____

Tuesday

_____

What God said to me:

_____

_____

_____

Wednesday

_____

What God said to me:

_____

Follow Me!

Thursday

What God said to me:

Friday

What God said to me:

Saturday

What God said to me:

_____

_____

_____

SESSION 4

CONNECTING TO THE BODY OF CHRIST, A LOCAL CHURCH

An old pastor once told of a young couple who came to him for premarital counseling. As he led them through various topics of discussion, he asked them to write vows, signifying something they promised to do as part of their marriage. At their next meeting, the groom-to-be read his vows, stating that he promised to honestly evaluate their relationship after two years, to see whether they should stay married. The bride-to-be was shocked! She said that their vows were for a lifetime. Her fiancé blurted out, "You don't believe in all that 'till death do us part' junk, do you?"

That exchange revealed a significant difference of opinion as to how the two young people viewed marriage. It should come as no surprise that they decided not to marry after that.

The perspective that God Almighty reveals to us as to how He operates in the world through the human beings whom He has saved includes team involvement. Jesus Christ's team or body is called the church. "Lone Ranger" Christians will generally burn out and fall by the wayside without someone to help them, hold them accountable, and encourage them to "walk worthy of the Lord, fully pleasing Him, being fruitful in every good work and increasing in the knowledge of God" (Colossians 1:10).

Read Ecclesiastes 4:9-12 and see what you can learn concerning the value of being together with others – and gathering together as a church.

- Why are two better than one?

- Is this only speaking on a human level?

- Verse 12 talks first about one, then two, then three. Who might the third one be when we are talking about church?

- Check out Jesus' statement about the church prevailing against hell itself in Matthew 16:18. How does this go with Ecclesiastes 4:9-12?

_____

_____

As a Christian, you must understand that your life on earth is symbiotically interconnected with a great network of other sentient, living beings. (Whoa, dude, that wording is, like, so organically ecological!) Your life—physically and spiritually—is woven together with others like the fibers of a rope or threads of a tapestry. You cannot live as a Christian on your own.

First, you are connected to God through Jesus Christ. Jesus said that you are like a branch that draws sap—life itself—from the vine on which it grows. If a branch is cut off the vine, it does not keep growing. Instead it immediately begins to die (John 15:1-8). Jesus went so far as to make the claim that without Him you can do *nothing* (John 15:5). Did He mean you can't even breathe or stand up without Him? Yes! God said in Colossians 1:16-17, "All things were created through Him [Christ] and for Him. And He is before all things, and in Him all things consist [hold together]." If

Jesus Christ withdrew His presence from you, you would immediately cease to exist. Read Galatians 2:20 and see how intimately your life depends on Jesus Christ.

Second, your life is connected with the rest of the church, which the Apostle Paul calls the body of Christ (Ephesians 1:22-23). The Apostle Peter labels the church as "living stones, [that] are being built up a spiritual house" (1 Peter 2:5). Hebrews names the church "the general assembly and church of the firstborn who are registered in heaven" (Hebrews 12:23). You are part of a living body of believers who have the life of Almighty God flowing through them and whose existence transcends, that is, extends beyond the borders of this physical universe into the spiritual realm that knows no limits! Jesus calls you a child of God (John 1:12-13). Your life is closely bound up with the Lord Jesus and those who have everlasting life through Him.

Many years ago, people burned coal in the furnaces in their homes. The coal burned until the remains became what people called "clinkers." They would shovel those rock-hard clinkers into a metal bucket and dispose of them into the potholes in their gravel driveways. Clinkers were never hot in the driveway because they would burn out relatively quickly when separated from the fire in the furnace.

If you get separated from the place the Almighty God meets with His people—that is, the church— you will not hold your fire very long. As you lay in the cold driveway of the world, whatever fire God lit within you will quickly be extinguished. Inertia from the physical world always overtakes a moving object when the object is not consistently propelled by some power source.

We get our power from Jesus Christ the Head through His body, which is the local church. That is the way Jesus operates in the world and it is His plan for reaching the world.

SEVEN SUPERNATURAL CONTACT POINTS IN THE LOCAL CHURCH

Many people who profess to be Christians, say they do not need to "go to church" because they can worship God and pray just as well all by themselves. That thinking is faulty. Remember, you are a disciplined disciple. You follow the commands of Jesus Christ of Nazareth because you love Him. Your goal as His disciple is to bear fruit as you live out the mission on which He sent you (John 15:14-16).

You are now on a mission from God. To accomplish that mission, you need a local church. At the same time, the local church to which the Holy Spirit leads you needs you.

Seven powerful activities exist, in which believers participate in the local church. As a matter of fact, these supernatural contact points connect Christ and His church. More than seven exist, but these seven are extremely vital. These contact points are like switches in an electrical circuit. When the switch is closed, contact occurs, and electricity flows through the entire circuit, bringing power to the place of intended purpose. But when the switch is open, no contact is made and the flow of electricity stops.

So it is in the church when believers engage in these seven crucial activities together. Contact is made with Jesus Christ and the power of God flows through the church so that the Holy Spirit accomplishes His purpose and will in the world.

Here is a list of Seven Supernatural Contact Points and a brief explanation of each.

SUPERNATURAL CONTACT POINT #1: Praise and Worship of God. You derive specific benefits from praise and worship. Psalm 22:3 states God is enthroned on the praises of His people. If you want to enthrone the Lord God in your life, praise Him. As you praise God, you will see your life circumstances in a new light. Situations you previously thought impossible or unbearable become workable through the power of the Holy Spirit. As you change, your circumstances change, and your life changes. Those are all the results of praising God.

Worship, on the other hand, is somewhat different than praise. Worship literally means to bow down to the ground as a demonstration of reverence and submission. Christians stand in awe, bow in reverence, and kneel in genuine adoration before the "Lord God Almighty, who was and is and is to come!" (Revelation 4:8).

Jesus said that God the Father has launched an all-out search across time and space to find people who truly worship Him in their spirits. He went on to say, "God is Spirit, and those who worship Him must worship in spirit and truth" (John 4:23-24).

You will find you are healthier, happier, better adjusted, and better equipped to face the struggles of life when you worship and praise God in spirit and truth.

SUPERNATURAL CONTACT POINT #2: Sharing God's Word for Faith. The Bible—especially the New Testament—presents a number of passages and verses that command God's children to preach the gospel, that is, to share God's word in the world. Each of the four gospels contains a commission by Jesus Christ Himself, sending out His disciples into the world to share His gospel (Matthew 28:19-20; Mark 16:15, Luke 24:46-47; & John 20:21).

Take a look at Romans 10:14-17. Paul lays out a rather convincing argument in these verses. He asks the following rhetorical questions:

1) How can people call on Jesus Christ the Son of God if they have never believed in Him [or believed He existed]?
2) How can they believe in Jesus Christ if they have never heard of Him?
3) How will they hear about Jesus Christ if no one preaches [proclaims the gospel] to them?
4) How will preachers go out unless someone [a church, a body of believers] sends them?

Paul's conclusion that he draws is in verse 17: "So then faith comes by hearing, and hearing by the word of God." In this conclusion there are two jobs being done: the human job—preaching, and the God job—giving faith through the proclamation of the word. This does not mean you have to holler at people on a street corner. Whether you teach a Bible study or share a Bible verse with a hurting friend, you are preaching the gospel.

When we declare to the world—and to each other—the great things God has done and is doing through Jesus Christ,

God gives faith to those who respond positively to this proclamation. That is how we win souls and plunder the gates of hell. Believers preach. Sinners believe. Jesus Christ saves. The Holy Spirit regenerates. God is glorified. Ephesians 2:8-9 is fulfilled: "For by grace you have been saved through faith, and that not of yourselves; it is the gift of God, not of works, lest anyone should boast."

SUPERNATURAL CONTACT POINT #3: A Pastor to Shepherd the Sheep (Believers). Jesus was very clear about the fact that the church needs godly leaders. He not only sets the church in order, designating which leaders are to serve where, but He also defines the qualifications and character for those who lead. In addition, Jesus molds willing disciples into courageous and faith-filled leaders who can lead others to God's preferred future.

Look at Ephesians 4:1-16. In verses 1-6, the Holy Spirit shows us that every Christian—not only the pastor—is called to minister in and through the church. In order to make ministry a successful and fruitful reality, Christ gives gifts to His disciples. Verse 11 proclaims that "He Himself [Christ] gave some to be apostles, some prophets, some evangelists, and some pastors and teachers." Jesus Himself gave a gift to the church called pastors, which is another word for shepherds. If you study out verses 12-16, you will see that the pastor's job is to equip you— the saints (yes, you are a saint of God by virtue of your new spiritual birth)—for the work of ministry to which God called you and to edify or build up the church, the body of Christ.

The goal for all this equipping and edification is seen in verses 13-16. Individual saints (believers) as well as the whole church are expected to mature and grow in faith to become more like Jesus Christ the Lord. The goal of a good shepherd is to raise up the lambs to become full grown sheep.

Sometimes, Christians begin to think they don't need a pastor to lead them. But, Jesus Christ offers them this gift to mature, grow, and develop them into power-filled, devil-conquering, soul-winning ministers of the gospel. (Check out James 1:21-25 to see that our heavenly Father wants you to be a "doer of the word.")

This Contact Point can get difficult because relationships can sometimes become strained. Patience, wisdom, and forgiveness are needed. That is the reason God talks about the relationship of Jesus Christ with His church as a marriage. Read Ephesians 5:22-33, where God explains that it is not a slave/master relationship, but rather a love relationship between husband and wife.

SUPERNATURAL CONTACT POINT #4: Fellowship with Other Believers. Webster's dictionary definition of fellowship is: coming together as one – a mutual sharing of interests, purpose and activities – binding together in a partnership.

The church is the family of God. Luke 20:36, John 1:12, Romans 8:16, Galatians 5:6, and 1 John 3:2, along with many other New Testament verses make the point that Christians are children of God by virtue of their spiritual rebirth. God the Father makes them brothers and sisters when He gives them spiritual birth by grace through faith in Jesus Christ (Ephesians 2:8) and by the regenerating work of His Holy Spirit (Titus 3:5). Jesus Christ is also head of His church and disciples follow His leadership (Colossians 1:18 & Ephesians 1:22-23). (See also 1 John 1:3, 1 Corinthians 1:9, and 2 Corinthians 13:14.)

Fellowship is a bond—a glue—that holds you all together as you move forward in a common purpose. You are on a mission from God. Along the way, you will share joys and sorrows. You care about the lives of one another, strengthen others when they are weak, and accept help from others when you feel faint. You hold one another accountable, making sure you do not fall into sin, quit, or walk away from Christ altogether. Encouragement plays a huge role as you call yourselves to a higher standard in Jesus Christ than where you are right now. That is the reason Hebrews 10:24-26 says to "consider one another to stir up love and good works, not forsaking the assembling of ourselves together, ... exhorting one another, and so much the more as you see the Day approaching."

The core of fellowship is God's agape love. Trust others to have your best interest at heart. Just as Jesus Christ did for you, so always seek God's best for the other person.

SUPERNATURAL CONTACT POINT #5: Assignment and Anointing for Ministry. Jesus Christ has ordained and anointed the pastor and leadership team with the vision—the big picture—of what He wants to accomplish in that particular church body. Seeing the big picture also allows the leaders to know what needs to be done where.

It is similar to the builder looking at a set of blueprints to know which subcontractor to bring in at the correct time. One has to pour the concrete foundation first, then another builds the frame of the house on top of that. Carpenters must nail up the two-by-four studs before others can put up the drywall. So it is with the church—the right task being completed at the right time by the right people.

Read and study Titus 1:1-9 & 2:15. Do you see Jesus Christ's order expressed for the church in this passage?

Christ called, commissioned, and commanded Paul—Saul of Tarsus—to be His apostle. Paul then selects, appoints, and commands Titus to oversee the church on the island of Crete. Pastor Titus in turn selects and appoints elders in the local churches that meet in the cities and towns of Crete to assure that the gospel of Jesus Christ is being spread and having full reign in the lives of believers.

When the pastor assigns, deploys, and equips you to serve in a particular capacity, the plan of Jesus Christ will be successful. That is what Jesus promised in Matthew 16:18.

So, where does it say that the pastor assigns people to ministry? Look at Ephesians 4:11-12. The pastor has two main tasks here: equipping and edifying. Equipping has to do with strapping in and suiting up participants for participation. Edifying has to do with building people up so they live and work confidently.

Here are three Bible passages to keep in mind as you serve in the ministry to which you are called, assigned, and anointed: Colossians 1:9-12, Colossians 3:17, and Philippians 4:8-9 & 13. These verses will keep your eyes focused on Jesus Christ, your feet following the path of His word, your hands doing the work of His will, and your mind steady on His great and precious promises (2 Peter 1:4).

SUPERNATURAL CONTACT POINT #6: Practicing the Use of Spiritual Gifts. The guidelines and expectations which Jesus Christ places upon His church for the use of spiritual gifts can be found in Romans 12:1-9 and 1 Corinthians 12-14. In Romans 12:1-9, the words God uses reveal that the gifts are not used for the exaltation of one individual. Paul uses the words "we," "members," and "us"—all plurals—to let us know that God gives these gifts to the whole body of Christ through individual Christians.

The passage found in 1 Corinthians 12-14 carries much of the teaching specific for the use of spiritual gifts. When you look at this passage, notice that Chapter 13—right in the middle—defines what holds the church together when everyone ministers according to the anointing of the Holy Spirit: agape love. That is God's highest form of love that always seeks the best for the other person, and while doing so, also gains God's best for oneself.

1 Corinthians 12-14 also provides several key lessons about spiritual gifts. First, the Holy Spirit gives at least one spiritual gift to each Spirit-filled believer (1 Cor. 12:7). Second, these spiritual gifts are given to build up the whole church (1 Cor. 12:7). That doesn't mean the only place you can use them is in the church building. The goal and purpose of the Holy Spirit is to build up His people, the church. Third, the Holy Spirit gives the gifts according to His will for the church and for the individual believer. Fourth, God puts a limit on how many should speak out during gathering times, in those times we call worship services. Fifth, people can control the use of the gift, for good or ill (1 Cor. 12:32). Sixth, services or gatherings should not be chaotic, confusing, and distracting. They are to be well-ordered and self-controlled according to the standards set by each individual church body in order to honor the Lord Jesus Christ.

The use of spiritual gifts builds up the church, making it stronger in the Spirit, giving confidence among fellow Christians who love God and one another with agape love.

Practice your spiritual gift(s). If you are not sure which gift you have, study these Bible passages with your mentor or pastor and discuss it with them. Then try it and see how you do. You may make mistakes. It's okay. Dedicate yourself to hearing Jesus' voice and following the lead of His Holy Spirit.

SUPERNATURAL CONTACT POINT #7: Pooling Resources to Increase the Fruit. In the movie, "The Princess Bride" (©1987, 20th Century Fox), Inigo, Fezzik, and Westley prepare to storm the castle of the evil Prince Humperdinck in order to save Westley's true love, Princess Buttercup. The sixty men who guard the gate stand between the three heroes and their mission.

Westley asks, "And our assets?" to which Inigo replies, "Your brains, Fezzik's strength, my steel." After a moment Westley exclaims, "If only we had a wheelbarrow, that would be something!" Fezzik and Inigo declare that they left one not far away. Westley mutters, "Well, why didn't you list that among our assets in the first place?" Then Westley states, "What I wouldn't give for a holocaust cloak!" Inigo admits, "There we cannot help you." But Fezzik surprisingly pulls one out of his shirt, asking, "Will this do?" With the wheelbarrow, the holocaust cloak, and a lit candle (which they also did not list among their assets), the three friends storm the castle, drive away the guards, and rescue Princess Buttercup.

"And our assets?"

What resources are available to you—to your body of believers—in the church to make the mission of Jesus Christ a reality? Some churches think they do not have much available to fulfill God's vision for the body of Christ.

Read John 6:1-14. When Jesus decides to feed the people (about 5000 men), Andrew tells Jesus that there is a boy with a lunch of five dinner rolls and two small fish. Andrew then adds, "But what are they among so many?" (v. 9). Andrew thinks the resources available to Jesus are inadequate to meet the demands of the people. But in the hands of Jesus Christ the Son of God, those loaves and fishes become enough for all those people. In fact, they pick up twelve baskets full of leftovers (v. 13).

What resources, what assets are at your disposal in your local church? You might want to make an actual list of the people, talents, skills, gifts, experiences, physical facilities, location, and any other assets your local church possesses. In the hands of Jesus Christ, these assets which are given to you can become a potent force to achieve the mission to which you are called.

Beware of becoming too dependent on the material resources of the church. Remember that your faith and trust are in the Lord Jesus Christ, not in the goods your church owns. Check out Jesus' warning to the Laodicean church in Revelation 3:14-22.

How do you utilize and direct those resources? Are your priorities in line with the values, mission, and priorities of Jesus Christ the Head of the church? Three good indicators of what your church values most are: what it spends its money on, what it celebrates, and where it invests its time.

Brother and Sister in Christ, the last days of history are upon the church, as the Bible says. (For example, see 2 Timothy 3:1; Hebrews 1:2; James 5:3; 1 Peter 1:5 & 20; 2 Peter 3:3; 1 John 2:18; & Jude 18.) Because time is growing short, plan the work that God has laid before you. Focus your energy, sharpen your tools, and make time to work at the harvest.

You may not think you have much to offer, but you do make a difference. Don't spend less time at church; spend more time in the house of God. That way you will be built up for ministering in the world. Don't withhold finances from the ministry; tithe and give offerings and gifts as God puts them into your hands. As you work hard, pray for God to prosper you financially in the world so that you may have more to sow into the kingdom work of God. Don't slack off your efforts to minister; fully plunge yourself into ministering in order to win souls to Christ and to build up other believers. Pour everything that God has poured into you—both material and spiritual gifts—into His harvest work of the kingdom.

Also remember that, because it is God who works through you and through the church, you cannot lose. God told us so in Luke 10:17-20, John 16:33, Romans 8:31-39, 1 Corinthians 15:57, 2 Corinthians 2:14, James 4:7-10, 1 Peter 5:6-11, 1 John 5:4-5, and Revelation 21:7. When you study these verses, you will see that Jesus Christ has already provided the victory for you. Therefore, just do what He called you to do – and you will not lose, rather you will win.

Stand firm. Stay in church. Study God's word. Obey Jesus. Pray in the Holy Spirit. Do these things and you will be fruitful in your walk with Him.

SESSION 5

FOLLOWING YOUR PASTOR – YOUR SHEPHERD

The New Testament in the Bible is comprised of twenty-seven books. Of those twenty-seven books, at least thirteen were written by Saul of Tarsus, a.k.a., the Apostle Paul. (Many church scholars are not certain as to whether Paul wrote the Epistle to the Hebrews. If he did, then that would make the total he penned fourteen. Another interesting fact is the reason Paul has two names. Saul is his Hebrew or Jewish name and Paul is his Latin or Roman name.)

Having been used by God to write about half of the New Testament might lead most people today to imagine that Paul had some kind of rock star status in the early church. But Chapter 9 of the book of Acts of the Apostles reveals two episodes in the life of Saul as he converted to Christianity.

In Acts 9, as Saul meets Jesus Christ on the road to Damascus, Jesus commands him to go to into that city and await further instructions. For the next three days, as Saul fasts and prays, God gives him a vision of a man named

Ananias coming to pray over him. Then the Lord speaks to Ananias, a Christian, to go to the house where Saul was staying and to pray over him as Saul was now a believer.

Here is where it gets interesting. Ananias has heard the warnings about why Saul came to Damascus. Saul came to arrest and kill Christians. Could this be nothing more than a ploy to draw Christians out of hiding to capture them? Ananias raises his fears to the Lord in prayer.

But God knew the truth and immediately responded, "Go, for he is a chosen vessel of Mine, to bear my name before Gentiles, kings, and the children of Israel" (v. 15).

Because Ananias was an obedient, faithful servant of Jesus Christ, he did what God commanded. He prayed over Saul, welcomed him into the church, then introduced him to the other believers.

Sometime later, when Saul made it back to Jerusalem, he tried to meet with the Christians there. But, they did not believe he was a changed man, though they had heard stories about his conversion. It took another brave soul, Barnabas, to take a risk on Saul's behalf. Barnabas took Saul to see the apostles, the leaders of the church. His introduction, testimony about Saul's conversion and ministry, and willingness to vouch for Saul paved the way for Saul's acceptance throughout the church.

Even the great Apostle Paul needed someone to lead him to where God wanted him to be.

You might be good at many things. But, as a new Christian, you need someone to help you reach your God-intended potential. That person is your pastor.

The good news is that Jesus Christ already knows what you need. To fulfill that need, He gave you a pastor as a special gift, both for you and for your church.

Here is a good study for you to learn about how much Jesus loves and values you, your church, and your pastor. Turn to Ephesians 4:1-16.

Verse 1 states that you are to "walk worthy of the calling with which you were called." In other words, Jesus Christ called you into His kingdom and His church. Now you have a ministry or service to do. So ... get busy. Get to work doing whatever Jesus gives you to do. Only make sure you do it as well as you are able for the Lord Himself.

Do you know what your ministry is? Write down what God called you to do.

_____

_____

Verses 2-6 reminds you that you don't "do" church all by yourself. You are not in ministry in a vacuum. Learn to live and serve in harmony with the whole body. In addition, every Christian will give an account of his or her service to Jesus Christ, the Head of the church.

How does your service work in harmony and synchronization with all the other ministers in the church?

_____

_____

Verse 7 mentions a gift from Jesus Christ. Verse 8 quotes Psalm 68:18 about the gifts He gives to people on earth. Then verse 11 lists five ministry gifts that Jesus Christ Himself gives to the church. Don't confuse these five gifts from Jesus in Ephesians 4 with the spiritual gifts (charismata) from the Holy Spirit in 1 Corinthians 12:1-11 or the gifts given by God the Father in Romans 12:3-8.

These gifts in Ephesians 4 are gifts or offices given to the church to make specific things happen for every believer. These are called Five-Fold Ministry gifts. Take a look at these in your Bible.

Read verses 11-12. List the five-fold ministry gifts below.

1. _____

2. _____

3. _____

4. _____

5. _____

Now list the two tasks of the five-fold minister that benefit and bless the saints, the body of Christ from verse 12.

1. _____

2. _____

These five ministry offices are quite important to the church because they are important to Jesus Christ. He is the church's wisdom (1 Corinthians 1:30). So, He knows what Christians need even more than they do.

What do these five-fold ministers do? Apostles start, pioneer, and lead churches where there are none. They make sure those churches stay on track with Jesus and His word. Prophets exhort and encourage believers and churches, and when there is a need, they bring correction. Evangelists call sinners to repentance and to believe in Jesus Christ. Teachers instruct and train believers in the biblical doctrines of the church.

So, what does your pastor do?

The word "pastor" comes from the word "shepherd." God revealed in the Bible that His people are like sheep and that He intends to shepherd them. He does that through the pastor of a church, who Jesus gives as a gift. Jesus calls Himself the Good Shepherd in John 10 in order to set the pattern of what a good shepherd or pastor is and what he does. That is the pattern the pastor follows.

When you go to a see a doctor for a medical problem, you may notice that doctor is sometimes referred to a "specialist," with special training in a specific field. These doctors go through many years of schooling. Think about it. They attend kindergarten through 12th grade (thirteen years), college (four years), medical school (four years), then residency (three to four years). After several years of medical practice, they can seek further education to become certified in their field of expertise (at least two to four more years). That's twenty-seven to twenty-nine years of formal education just to be considered a "specialist."

If you do a thorough search through the Bible on what God says is the role of the pastor/shepherd, you will make an amazing discovery. You will find three major tasks in the Bible that God wants His shepherds to do well.

First, God expects His pastor/shepherds to *lead or guide* His sheep, that is, His people. That means the pastor talks to God, finds out where God wants His people to go, and then takes the people, the congregation in that direction. The pastor is the leader. The people are the followers. You can see why the apostles insisted on focusing on prayer and study of the word of God in Acts 6:1-7. Their connection with the Lord through prayer is the lifeline for the entire church. If they dared sever that lifeline in order to do other tasks, the whole congregation would suffer terribly, perhaps even die. And that is not overstating the case.

Second, God expects His pastor/shepherds to *feed or provide* for His people. The feeding that Christians need is from the Word of God. Pastors must preach the gospel and teach the doctrines of God's Word. Pastors cannot simply teach popular cultural beliefs or political views. God expects His children to mature in the faith, to strap up for world-changing ministry, and prepare to battle the spiritual principalities and powers at work in the world (Ephesians 4:11-16, 6:10-20). In order to accomplish this great mission and to prevent spiritual malnourishment, pastors must feed Christians a steady diet of God's word, the ultimate power food.

Third, God expects His pastor/shepherd to *protect or guard* His people. The church is under attack today. God has put a leader out in front who will protect the sheep from predators and robbers. Pastors must possess the qualities of fearlessness, courage, and a willingness to fight for what is right. In John 10:11-12, Jesus said that a good shepherd will sacrifice his own life to save the sheep. But the hired hand doesn't care much for the sheep. It's just a job to him. So, at the first sign of danger, he runs for safety, leaving the sheep to fend for themselves. God's pastors are not hired hands, but rather good shepherds according to the standards set by Jesus Christ Himself.

Here are two side points that are worth considering:

1) Too many pastors shy away from strong preaching and teaching of the Bible because they fear what people in their congregations will say or do as a result. Check out what Jesus has to say about fearing people in Luke 12:4-5 and in Matthew 5:11-12. Many of the great Christian renewal movements of the past are dying long, slow deaths because their pastors have quit seeking God and preaching His word. Instead they seek to keep people happy or comfortable in their unsaved or backslidden state.
2) Too many Christians quit church or jump from church to church using the excuse that they are "not being fed." While that sounds very spiritual, it falls more into the category of people's attitude in the last days of history, which God describes in 2 Timothy 4:3-4. The antidote for this is presented clearly in the preceding verses, 2 Timothy 3:16-4:2.

Pray for your pastor, that God's word and the Holy Spirit's anointing will flow freely.

Read 2 Timothy 3:16-4:5. Notice that in verse 4:2, God commands pastors to "convince, rebuke, exhort." Convince, here, does not mean to persuade. It is the same word used in

John 16:8 for the Holy Spirit convicting people that they are in sin. Rebuke is a sharp scolding, which means correction is in order. Exhortation is strong encouragement, as if a coach is vigorously shouting for an athlete to push to the limit to reach the finish or goal line.

EXPECTATIONS

Many people who participate in churches, including those who are guests or visitors, have some expectations of pastors. For example, even when people attend a church wedding, they have certain expectations of how the pastor, clergy, or licensed "officiant" will dress, act, speak, etc. The same can be said when people attend a funeral.

Understand, then, that when you participate in your local church, you have expectations of your pastor. Some may be biblical, others may not. In order for the church to operate at its peak effectiveness, everyone—from the pastor to the last person in—should at least be in the process of bringing their thoughts and expectations into line with the word of God. After all, Jesus Christ is the head of the church. Therefore, He sets the standards. "We are His people, and the sheep of His pasture" (Psalm 100:3).

The following points may help you examine your own thoughts and expectations. Take a look at what your pastor is not.

1. Your pastor is not your employee or your personal assistant. Do not think that because you contribute tithes and offerings that you pay his or her salary and, therefore, have the right to boss him or her around. Your pastor does not work for you. He or

she is an undershepherd for the Lord Jesus Christ. So, don't expect your pastor to do your bidding or work of ministry.
2. Your pastor is not your personal, private, or family chaplain. When you experience a bump in the road of life, you should not expect your pastor to drop everything else and ignore everyone else to be with you. As your pastor builds you up and prepares you for your ministry, you should become stronger to serve before the Lord. That doesn't mean the pastor is too good or too busy to minister to you in times of need. But, don't expect your pastor constantly to be at your personal beck and call. You are growing stronger to handle the bumps and struggles of life in the Lord's strength (Col. 1:11).
3. Your pastor is not your personal buddy. It is not that pastors can't be friends with the sheep of the flock. But, often familiarity blurs the lines of respect and expectation. That means that friends often begin to expect special treatment that no one else receives. Remember the old adage: "Familiarity breeds contempt." Jesus Christ placed your pastor in that office for your good, to help you grow in the Spirit. Remember that part of your pastor's job is to "convince, rebuke, exhort with all longsuffering and teaching" (2 Tim. 4:2). So, being buddies with your pastor may not be to your greatest spiritual advantage.

Pastors are vital to the survival of disciples. Here is how your pastor helps you become a better disciple and gives you what you need to thrive as you prepare to meet your Lord in these last days.

First, your pastor prays. Your pastor talks to and intercedes with God the Father on your behalf daily—constantly. These prayers throw out the lifeline that brings aid to you in time of need and provides the safety net to protect you (Ps. 91); send angels on heavenly assignments to you (Heb. 1:14); help set up divine appointments and call for Christ's wisdom when you need it (James 1:5). In Acts 6:1-7, the apostles followed the Holy Spirit's leading and instructed the church that their focus was to "give ourselves continually to prayer and to the ministry of the word" (Acts 6:4).

Second, your pastor preaches and teaches the word of God. He or she spends much time praying over and studying the meaning of the Scriptures so that messages delivered to you come from heaven. God speaks to you through your pastor. It is to your advantage to take notes and/or get recordings of your pastor's messages to listen to repeatedly so that you can learn everything you can from the Bible. God may open a new revelation, speak a word of correction, confirm a direction for your life, or affirm you because you are so pleasing to Him. Listen to your pastor and your faith in Jesus Christ will grow and stretch. God said, "Faith comes by hearing, and hearing by the word of God" (Rom. 10:17). You will be blessed and helped in life and prepared for eternal life when you pay attention to your pastor's preaching and teaching.

Third, your pastor prophesies and speaks the truth in love to "upgrade" the lives of the disciples under his or her care. Read Heb. 12:5-11 to see how important discipline is to a son or daughter of God. 2 Corinthians says that a Christian is a new creation and the old person is passed away. But, old habits and patterns of life may take time to change. Prophesying and speaking truth in love through the pastor is one of God's ways to help fix the problems you face (called sanctification). A supernatural word to you through your pastor will help you focus on Jesus (not on the person of the pastor). It will also kick start your Christian life on God's highway of holiness (Is. 35:8-10).

Fourth, your pastor sees the big picture, the vision the Holy Spirit showed him for your local church. As the undershepherd of Jesus Christ, it is God the Holy Spirit who imparts the vision of where He wants the church to go, what He wants it to be, how He wants it to minister in the world. When your pastor rightly expresses that vision, the Holy Spirit confirms it in the hearts of the believers. People who live in fear and doubt will always exist. But, those who listen will hear the confirmation of the Holy Spirit in their hearts.

When Nehemiah spoke God's vision of rebuilding the walls of Jerusalem, the people replied, "Let us rise up and build" (Neh.2:18). Your church will flourish when Ephesians 2:11-16 is in full God-ordained operation.

Fifth and finally, based on the vision from Jesus Christ, your pastor strategically organizes the work of ministry for the saints. Because the pastor sees the big picture and the people of the church, he knows what needs to be done and who should do it. Your pastor may need help working out the details as to how something should be done. That is the reason God brings people with different talents, skills, and levels of expertise into the church. One person cannot do it all. Much more can be accomplished when many hands share in the work. The Holy Spirit also gives spiritual gifts into the believers—the church—so that the whole church may grow in health and maturity, becoming more like Christ. Look at Acts 6:1-7 again to see how the apostles stayed within their calling and helped others fulfill their calling. Also check out Heb. 13:7-8, 17 and Col. 3:17 to see how to keep your heart right with God within your local church.

As you read through the verses, did the Holy Spirit bring to your mind words you have spoken or deeds you have done that were short of His mark outlined in His word? Repent of those now, asking God to forgive you. Then make note of those so as not to repeat them.

_____

_____

_____

_____

_____

Did the Holy Spirit ignite your passion to become engaged in some ministry in the church or to start a new ministry within the church? Make note of those so as to remember to talk with your pastor about them.

_____

_____

_____

_____

_____

Jesus Christ has purposely given your pastor as a gift to you to help you reach your highest potential in serving Him. Make the most of that gift. Draw on the anointing of the Holy Spirit that is flowing through your pastor. Always seek to honor and bless your pastor and never become a thorn in his or her side. God blesses you through your pastor. Therefore, be a blessing in return.

LESSON 6

SPIRIT-LED LIVING

    The story is told of an old Christian who went off to live in the wilderness around the Dead Sea about 400 years after Jesus Christ walked the earth. One day, a rather rugged looking, but richly clothed man came upon the Christian as the man of God knelt in prayer.

    Looking up, the Christian said kindly, "How may I help you?"

    The man stepped forward, hands on his hips, chin jutting, with chest puffed out, and declared, "I am Galba, the most feared bandit east of the Great Sea." Then he paused to see what effect his introduction would have upon the Christian.

    Without rising, moving, or changing expressions, the Christian asked softly, "What is it that you seek?"

    The bandit changed in front of the Christian's eyes. His bravado evaporated as he sighed deeply, slumped his shoulders, and hung his head down. When he tried to speak, his voice cracked with emotion. He began to weep as his story tumbled out. "I possess more wealth than I could have ever imagined. In my life of banditry these past five and twenty years, I have killed many men, have stolen the goods of many houses, caravans, and ships, and have taken and sold many men, women, and children as slaves. But, with all this, I have no peace. My spirit within me is filled with wretchedness. And though I have mocked your God in the past, I now come to ask you to help me find eternal life and the peace that passes understanding."

The Christian stood and faced the man. "How do you propose to learn the ways of the Lord Jesus Christ?"

The bandit held out both hands, "My brother, let me be your disciple. Allow me to follow wherever you go, so that I may learn all that you know. And if I cannot be your disciple, then I will serve you as a slave. Please let me follow you!"

After thinking for a minute, the Christian asked, "You say you have killed many men, stolen many goods, and enslaved many people?"

"Yes, that is true. I cannot deny it."

"Then you may follow me on one condition."

"Name it! I will do whatever it is you say."

"Good," smiled the old Christian. "That is my condition: that you do whatever I say."

Galba the Bandit was overjoyed and smiled with delight.

For his part, the Christian simply turned and walked away. As the new disciple followed, he regaled the Christian with stories of his daring exploits, harrowing escapes, and swashbuckling adventures.

Suddenly, the Christian stopped and turned around. Pointing down, he commanded, "Pick up that rock and carry it."

Galba looked down at the sizable stone and asked, "Why? What do you need it for? And how far must I carry it?"

Turning abruptly, the Christian walked away, saying, "You must do whatever it is I say—or leave at once."

Without another word, Galba picked up the stone and followed his new master.

A few minutes later, the Christian repeated the scene with a second rock, then again with a third. This new disciple staggered under the weight of the three stones and panted heavily as he tried to keep up to the old Christian. So out of breath was the bandit that he could not continue with his stories.

After a while, they came to the base of a steep hill. The old Christian began to climb, using both hands and feet. Galba stood for a moment with furrowed brow, looking up the hill, still panting from his heavy load. He shifted all three stones into one arm. Then with great determination and a huge gulp of air, he began to climb.

Not far up, the disciple slipped and almost fell backward. As he caught himself, he cried out, "Brother! Save me!"

Looking down, the Christian said calmly, "Drop one of the rocks."

Immediately the bandit let one of the stones roll from his hand. It clattered and crashed all the way to the bottom, loosening dirt and rocks on its way. The bandit heaved a sigh of relief as he resumed his climb.

About halfway to the top he slipped once more, nearly falling to his death. Again he cried out for help.

Once again his mentor shouted down, "Drop one of the rocks."

Without hesitation the disciple obeyed and all seemed well.

But, as the bandit neared the top, his strength gave out and he could go no further. So, he called out to the Christian who by now waited for him at the summit.

Without even looking over the edge, the Christian called out, "Drop your last rock."

Gladly did the bandit unburden himself of his remaining stone. After a few minutes of catching his breath, he regained sufficient strength to make it to the top.

As he sat resting in the dirt with his rich frock tattered and dusty, he asked the Christian, "My brother, I do not understand. Why did you have me pick up and carry those three rocks? They nearly cost me my life!"

"You speak the truth," said the aged Christian. "In your old life, you killed many men, stole many goods, and enslaved many people. Yet, you carried those deeds as if they were something of which you should be proud. In truth, they are rocks that will cost you your life. Only you were too foolish to see it. I simply revealed it to you using those three large stones. The Lord Jesus taught us that no one can serve two masters. You cannot serve God and mammon. Unless you repent and drop those three rocks, you will not find eternal life—nor the peace which accompanies it."

SUPERNATURALLY NEW AND DIVINELY IMPROVED

Having believed in the Lord Jesus Christ, you are a new creation, different than you were before.

Look at 2 Corinthians 5:17. What three things does this verse say about you? Write them in the blanks below.

"If anyone [that's you] is in Christ, _____

_____."

"_____ have passed away."

"Behold, all things _____."

Now look at James 2:14-26. Concentrate your attention on verses 17 and 26. What two elements does it include about your new life in Christ? Write the answers below.

Verse 17 – "Thus also _____ by itself, if it does not have _____, is _____."

Verse 26 – "For as the body without the spirit is _____, so _____ without _____ is _____ also."

Therefore, if you are new, that means you are different. Just as you do not act the same way you did when you were two years old, you now think and act differently as a Christian than when you were a sinner. Jesus Christ lives in you. God the Holy Spirit has regenerated you (you are born again) and, if you asked God for it, you received the baptism of the Holy Spirit. That means you have power for living a holy life and to show people the way to Jesus Christ (to be a witness of what you experienced).

Therefore, because you are changed—transformed from within—you will show it by your actions. Just as an incandescent light bulb shines light out from the filament inside it, so your improved actions result from the holiness that is within you.

The Bible says that three forces try to stop you from following God: the world, the flesh, and the devil. (See 1 John 2:15-17 & 3:8.) You belong to Jesus Christ, having been purchased by His blood (1 Corinthians 6:20). Therefore, you will want to live in a way that honors the Lord God and demonstrates to the world around you that you belong to Him.

Three major actions, lifestyles, and attitudes prevail in the world today. Your life as a Christian will contrast with the world around you and make you stand out. These three actions are 1) how you speak (the words of your mouth), 2) how you control your body (healthy relationships and sexuality), and 3) how you handle money (earning and spending). Though many other attitudes and actions exist, these three stand out as most noticeable. So, it is important that you learn how to deal with these three.

YOUR MOUTH: Please learn these two important lessons about the words you speak.

1) The things you say reveal what is in your heart. Jesus said, "For out of the abundance of the heart the mouth speaks" (Matthew 12:34).

Years ago, at a marriage seminar, an older married couple shared about how they constantly joked about each other. The wife called her husband a "fat slob" and the husband called his wife an "old nag." One day they both realized something. He acted like a fat slob and she behaved like an old nag. They also noticed how unhappy they felt, and that people did not want to socialize with them anymore. That couple's "joking" was harmful to their marriage and to their relationships with others. They came to this conclusion: their words exposed their true thoughts and they were reaping the fruit of their words.

Your words reflect what is truly in your heart. Listen to yourself during the course of a day. Are you spewing out negative, demeaning, destructive words about yourself? About other people? About your job, your family, your school? Please don't think that you are being dishonest by holding back those negative words.

Seek to speak the truth and spiritual reality from God's perspective. This is true honesty.

In Romans 12:1-2 the Holy Spirit tells you to present your body as a living sacrifice, that is, get yourself in to your church's worship service. There you will hear the word preached and taught, worship in spirit and truth, and fellowship in love. By doing all that, your mind will be renewed, you will be transformed, and you will know and live in "that good and acceptable and perfect will of God." Change what is inside you so that what comes out of you is different.

2) The second lesson to learn is that your words create your future. Proverbs 18:21 states, "Death and life are in the power of the tongue, and those who love it will eat its fruit." Jesus also taught, "But I say to you that for every idle word men may speak, they will give account of it in the day of judgment. For by your words you will be justified, and by your words you will be condemned" (Matthew 12:36-37).

What you hear yourself say is what you will believe as the truth. You will then live that out in your life. A few years ago, a young man who was in ninth grade related to a friend that no one in his family had ever graduated from high school. He believed he would not. His friend encouraged him to be the first, asking him to imagine telling his grandchildren that he was the first in his family to get his diploma. The young man began to believe it was possible. But over the next year his father strongly reinforced the family "tradition." At the end of his sophomore year the young man dropped out of school. He accepted what he was told by his family. He then said what he believed and believed what he said.

Your words become reality. So, watch your mouth. What should you be saying? Speak the truth of God's word, the Bible. You will always be safe if you say what God says. Ephesians 5:26 says that Jesus Christ sanctifies and cleanses you "with the washing of water by the word." Stay in the word, in reading, studying, and declaring it so that you are changed by it. But, not only are you changed by speaking the word of God, your circumstances will also change.

Read Proverbs 10, Mark 11:22-26, and James 3:1-12 to see what God says about the fruit that comes from your words. (Also check out Appendix B at the end of this book. This provides a list of many things God says are true about you in His word.)

Write down one powerful thing God says about you in His word:

YOUR BODY: Understand that God created and designed the real you (your spirit) to rule over the rest of you, that is, to be in charge over your soul and your body.

You are comprised of three parts, similar to God. God is a Trinity—Father, Son, and Holy Spirit. You are a trinity—spirit, soul, and body (1 Thessalonians 5:23). Imagine yourself as a pyramid. The top third, the point, is the spirit. That is the part that connects with God. The middle third is the soul—the intellect, mind, will, and emotions—the part that people often call the psyche. The bottom third or the base is the body.

If you invert or turn over the pyramid and try to stand it on the point, it will tip over. When your body becomes your master, you are inverted—upside down—and your life will "tip over." This is true if the body or mind is taken over by addiction or a lopsided obsession with food, drugs, alcohol, or if possessed by the lust for sex.

Sexuality seems to saturate modern society. People and businesses use sex to sell products, to gain power over others, and to bolster a sense of self-worth. The problem is that this culture has inverted the pyramid.

You are created to fellowship with God. When your spirit connects with God through faith in Jesus Christ, you have a powerful relationship with a living Being. But your mind and your body try to take over and rule your life.

Because sexual images and messages are so prevalent in society, through social media, television, music, sports, advertising, and movies, you are unknowingly inundated, that is, flooded with these temptations. You may feel sexual urges within your body. Your mind turns to certain less-than-Godly thoughts. Society tells you to run with and act on those urges and temptations.

But as a Christian, you are not ruled by your body. (It may be helpful for you to say that out loud right now: "I am not ruled by my body. Jesus Christ is my Lord!")

Listen to what Jesus had to say about this topic. In Mark 4:24, Jesus warned, "Take heed what you hear." The same could be said for what you look at and watch. Be careful! Once you see something or listen to something, you can't "unsee" or "unhear" it. What's more, studies now reveal that viewing sexual (pornographic) images creates patterns in the viewer's brain similar to scars that are difficult to heal.

God also commands His children about their sexual relationships. 1 Corinthians 6:18 tells Christians, "Flee sexual immorality." The word for sexual immorality is "fornication." Many people believe that fornication includes only sexual intercourse. But the use of your body or another person's body for sexual purposes—like viewing, touching, or actual intercourse—comes under the heading of sexual immorality.

This warning from God is similar to that of a parent telling a child not to play on the highway or not to stick a butter knife in a light socket. The child may think it is fun and totally safe. But the parent knows the potential danger and, as a result, warns the child. God is not trying to ruin your fun, He is watching out for your health and safety from an eternal perspective.

God's plan is for you to keep yourself pure for service to Him and to reserve sexual activity for the one person whom you marry. In addition to that, you can honor God and show respect for yourself and other people by being honorable, respectful, courteous, and considerate. Jesus said, "Therefore, whatever you want men to do to you, do also to them, for this is the Law and the Prophets" (Matthew 7:12). This is known as The Golden Rule. Do you want people to treat you with respect and honor? Then do so to them in advance.

Looking for sex outside of marriage is quite self-centered because it is focused on how the other person provides pleasure to you. Concerning yourself with showing respect and honor to the other person is engaging the highest form of love revealed in the Bible: agape. This is the kind of love God extended to you when He sent His only begotten Son so that you might have everlasting life (John 3:16).

If you think you cannot control your sexual urges, then change your thinking to come into line with God's word. Study Philippians 4:13, Colossians 1:9-12, Mark 9:23 & 10:27, and Luke 1:37. God would never give you a command—like "Flee sexual immorality"—if you could not obey Him. He provides the strength, power, and desire to get it done according to His will. So, you can keep yourself clean and pure. The choice to do it is yours.

YOUR MONEY: Society teaches some powerful ideas about material possessions. Here are a few. First, people are taught to believe that the money they gain belongs to them. Second, if other people have more material possessions than you, they must be greedy and gain what they have at your expense. Third, the things that "rich" people have should be taken away and shared with everyone else. A fourth belief is that if the rich would just share their wealth, no one would suffer from poverty.

Jesus was also quite clear in His teachings concerning wealth: you are a steward—a caretaker or manager—of what God has given you. That means that the money you have and the things you possess do not actually belong to you. They belong to God, who is gracious enough to allow you to use them here on earth.

Why does wealth attract people so strongly? Gold, silver, and diamonds, for example, are no more than rocks mined from the earth. Rocks are inanimate objects. What or who gives these minerals such value? For many centuries, people have done almost anything to get their hands on these rocks. The Bible says King Solomon had so much gold that he ate and drank from utensils made only of that precious metal. The Roman emperor, Nero, built himself a palace covered with so much gold that he called it *Domus Aurea*, which is Latin for *Golden House*.

Jesus clearly warned His disciples about the dangers of wealth. He said, "No one can serve two masters; for either he will hate the one and love the other, or else he will be loyal to the one and despise the other. You cannot serve God and mammon" (Matthew 6:24). It is most interesting that Jesus talked about mammon as if it were a person, one who possesses the power to be master over another, to command and control the other's future or destiny. Why would Jesus talk about an inanimate object as if it were alive?

The truth of the matter is that Jesus is not just talking about money, either the paper, coin, or precious metal version. Look at Matthew 6:24 in different English translations, if you have them available to you. The last word, *mammon*, is translated *money* in the ESV and NIV, *mammon* in the KJV and NKJV, and *wealth* in the NASB. The reality is that mammon is not simply money or wealth.

Jesus talked about mammon as a personal entity because it is a spirit that threatens to take over people. The fact that this spirit of mammon does not come from God means that it is demonic. Do not let this frighten you or make you think that the bogeyman lives in your wallet, purse, or bank account. In fact, God wants to prosper you so that you can be a vital force in spreading the gospel of Jesus Christ. The devil wants to stop you from doing that.

How can you keep Jesus Christ as Lord of your whole life, including your finances? The first thing you do is tithe. That means you give one tenth (10%) to God. Let me share some specifics about tithing.

Why? Read Malachi 3:8-12. In this passage, the Lord God is having a strong discussion with the people of Israel, especially the leaders. God is calling them on their less-than-faithful behavior. He asks, "Will a man rob God?" The question implies that the robber thinks he will get away with the crime. Then God adds a charge against these leaders, "Yet you have robbed Me!"

In response, the leaders gasp, "In what way have we robbed You?!"

God has His answer ready, "In tithes and offerings" (v. 8). Tithing had been a commanded practice for the Israelites for more than a thousand years. So, God now gives them clear direction, "Bring all the tithes into the storehouse, that there may be food in My house" (v. 10). Since the days of Moses, the children of Israel—and now the disciples of Jesus Christ—provide for the work of ministry. God puts wealth in our hands and pockets "that there may be food in My house," that is, provision for a ministry base of operations.

Think of it this way. Let's say your mother gave you $25.00 to go to the pharmacy to buy her prescription medication. But on the way to the drug store, you stopped at the tavern and drank away the money. Your mother would have the right to say (in the words of God), "Yet, you have robbed me!" The money put into your hands was not yours, but hers. She had the right to dictate how you were to use it. You were simply the caretaker of the funds, the delivery person sent on a mission.

So it is with the tithe. God puts that money into your hands to bring into His house, the church, so that you and the other Christians will fund or provide for the work of ministry. If you spend the tithe on something else, you are robbing from God. God's question to the Jews in about 400 B.C. is the same question He asks you: "Can a man rob God [and get away with it]?"

Verse 9 is a little disconcerting and upsetting. Read it for yourself. God said, "You are cursed with a curse, for you have robbed Me." Notice God did *not* say that He is cursing you. The truth is, you are bringing it upon yourself.

Once a boy on the farm was helping to fix a wall on the barn. The boy accidentally hit his finger with the hammer as he nailed a board in place. He dropped the hammer and cried out in pain. One of men who was helping, smiled and asked, "Did that hurt?"

"Yes," the boy whimpered.

"Then don't hit your hand anymore," the man chuckled.

That may seem silly, but it is good advice. If what you are doing is hurting you or causing you to be cursed, stop doing it. If you want to be blessed in God's kingdom, then tithe.

It is God's choice to bless you. Look again at Malachi 3. Verse 10 says, "Try Me in this." This is the one place in the entire Bible where God gives us permission to test Him to see if His promises work. (Some people try to act all spiritual at this point, saying, "I would never test God.") But try tithing and watch God fulfill His promise in your bank account.

God promised that He will "open for you the windows of heaven and pour out for you such blessing that there will not be room enough to receive it" (v. 10). In other words, by giving God the tithe (10%) first, He will bless the other 90% so that you have more than you did with the original 100%. Mathematically that doesn't make sense. But, spiritually it always works.

Hold on a minute. (Or as they say in those TV infomercials, "But wait, there's more!") Verses 11 and 12 go on to give further promises. God Himself will rebuke the devourer. What is devouring your life, your finances, your body, your family, your career, or your sense of peace? God

Himself will rebuke—sharply scold it—and turn it away. These blessings are known as tither's rights. (And just so you know, this is God's idea to give you these rights as His child.)

How? How should you tithe? First. Do it first. Do not wait until all other bills are paid, you have taken a vacation, and gone shopping. Tithe first. Give to God what is due Him before you do anything else. As soon as you get paid, give God His tithe.

If you reason within your mind that you have to wait to see if you have enough left over after the bills are paid, then you have not learned God's lesson. Don't steal from God. Remember, He wants to bless you, so that "all nations call you blessed" (v. 12).

Some people debate whether the tithe should be on gross pay (before taxes, insurance, and other benefits are taken out) or net pay (after taxes, etc., are taken out). Don't get bogged down in a religious argument. Simply start out by tithing 10% of your take home pay. Once you establish the habit of tithing, ask the Lord about increasing it.

How else should you tithe? Malachi 3:10 says, "Bring all the tithes into the storehouse." In the days of Malachi (400 B.C.) many people bartered and traded using their crops, animals from their flocks and herds, and the goods they made and produced. Not many years ago, most people used cash or checks to buy what they needed. Today, most people use debit and credit cards and apps that tap into electronic banking. No one pays for their groceries or utility bills with a sheep or goat or a bushel of wheat.

The point of all this is that you may conduct all your business using electronic banking. If that is the case, then when you get paid, tithe to your church electronically. If your church doesn't accept electronic donations, ask if they will make it available. That way you tithe first to God.

But then, don't neglect to bring something in to the house of God when you go. You may have tithed electronically, but you can still bring a few dollars in cash to provide an offering, in addition to your tithe. Sacrifice for the body of Christ. A coffee at a coffee shop now costs $3.00 to $5.00 (in this locale). Give at least one cup of coffee a week to the Lord and for His kingdom. Jesus promised, "Seek first the kingdom of God and His righteousness, and all these things shall be added to you" (Matt. 6:33).

One more point about how to tithe. Always dedicate and consecrate your tithe to the Lord with prayer. Pray over your tithe and the church, which is the body of Christ. Call in the lost people who will believe as a result of your sowing into the kingdom work of the church. Pray for those who are and will be born again, water baptized, and Holy Spirit baptized. Pray over your pastor, your pastor's family, and the church staff. Also, do not neglect to claim the promises for yourself and your family as well. This is God's intention for you and for His church. Give it and pray it the way God means it.

What? The practice of tithing began about 2000 B.C. with Abraham. It was reaffirmed about 1500 B.C. through Moses when God commanded the Israelites through the Law. About 400 B.C. God again reaffirmed the practice with added blessings through the Prophet Malachi.

This has led to many modern-day Christians teaching that tithing is an Old Testament Jewish practice that died away with the advent of Jesus Christ of Nazareth. However, Jesus Himself commanded it in Matthew 23:23. You will also find an excellent explanation of tithing in Hebrews 7:1-19. Therefore, you can see that tithing is a New Testament church teaching and practice, complete with attached blessings from God Himself.

So, as the sports company said in their ads, just do it. Don't overthink it or try to find a loophole to get out of tithing. Just do it. This is exactly what God challenged the Jews to do through Malachi. "'Try Me now in this,' says the Lord of hosts" (Mal. 3:10). Take God at His word. You will have the same experience with God that caused King Solomon to pray, "There has not failed one word of all His good promise" (1 Kings 8:56).

Do your calculations here for your tithe.

How often do you get paid for your work?

_____

(This is how often you will then tithe.)

How much is your paycheck?

_____

Multiply that amount by .10 (10%).

_____ (your pay) x .10 =
_____ (tithe)

When you follow the Holy Spirit's leading, you will find strength for living, clarity of purpose, and wisdom in day-to-day decisions. You will walk according to the light of the Bible (Psalm 119:105) because the Holy Spirit never contradicts His word. Focus on pleasing your Lord and Savior Jesus Christ. Then you will have the peace that passes understanding.

EPILOGUE

You have just spent the last six (or more) weeks with a more experienced Christian learning to be a disciple of Jesus Christ. If you have not figured it out by now, a disciple is a student of Jesus Christ of Nazareth, who diligently studies His ways from His word and within His church, who yields to His Holy Spirit, and who looks forward to seeing His glorious return at any moment.

You are on the journey—this magnificent mission—that lasts beyond this lifetime into eternity.

It will not always be easy. There will be disappointments and difficulties. But the journey will always be worth it, so worth it! Don't let up. Don't quit. Stay strong. Stay connected.

"Now to Him who is able to do exceedingly abundantly above all that we ask or think, according to the power that works in us, to Him be glory in the church by Christ Jesus to all generations, forever and ever. Amen!" Ephesians 3:20-21.

APPENDIX A

READ THROUGH THE BIBLE IN ONE YEAR
from www.esv.org/biblereadingplans

January

- ☐ Jan. 1: Gen 1-2, Matt 1
- ☐ Jan. 2: Gen 3-5, Matt 2
- ☐ Jan. 3: Gen 6-8, Matt 3
- ☐ Jan. 4: Gen 9-11, Matt 4
- ☐ Jan. 5: Gen 12-14, Matt 5:1-26
- ☐ Jan. 6: Gen 15-17, Matt 5:27-48
- ☐ Jan. 7: Gen 18-19, Matt 6
- ☐ Jan. 8: Gen 20-22, Matt 7
- ☐ Jan. 9: Gen 23-24, Matt 8
- ☐ Jan. 10: Gen 25-26, Matt 9:1-17
- ☐ Jan. 11: Gen 27-28, Matt 9:18-38
- ☐ Jan. 12: Gen 29-30, Matt 10:1-23
- ☐ Jan. 13: Gen 31-32, Matt 10:24-42
- ☐ Jan. 14: Gen 33-35, Matt 11
- ☐ Jan. 15: Gen 36-37, Matt 12:1-21
- ☐ Jan. 16: Gen 38-40, Matt 12:22-50
- ☐ Jan. 17: Gen 41, Matt 13:1-32
- ☐ Jan. 18: Gen 42-43, Matt 13:33-58
- ☐ Jan. 19: Gen 44-45, Matt 14:1-21
- ☐ Jan. 20: Gen 46-48, Matt 14:22-36
- ☐ Jan. 21: Gen 49-50, Matt 15:1-20

- ☐ Jan. 22: Ex 1-3, Matt 15:21-39
- ☐ Jan. 23: Ex 4-6, Matt 16
- ☐ Jan. 24: Ex 7-8, Matt 17
- ☐ Jan. 25: Ex 9-10, Matt 18:1-20
- ☐ Jan. 26: Ex 11-12, Matt 18:21-35
- ☐ Jan. 27: Ex 13-15, Matt 19:1-15
- ☐ Jan. 28: Ex 16-18, Matt 19:16-30
- ☐ Jan. 29: Ex 19-21, Matt 20:1-16
- ☐ Jan. 30: Ex 22-24, Matt 20:17-34
- ☐ Jan. 31: Ex 25-26, Matt 21:1-22

February

- ☐ Feb. 1: Ex 27-28, Matt 21:23-46
- ☐ Feb. 2: Ex 29-30, Matt 22:1-22
- ☐ Feb. 3: Ex 31-33, Matt 22:23-46
- ☐ Feb. 4: Ex 34-36, Matt 23:1-22
- ☐ Feb. 5: Ex 37-38, Matt 23:23-39
- ☐ Feb. 6: Ex 39-40, Matt 24:1-22
- ☐ Feb. 7: Lev 1-3, Matt 24:23-51
- ☐ Feb. 8: Lev 4-6, Matt 25:1-30
- ☐ Feb. 9: Lev 7-9, Matt 25:31-46
- ☐ Feb. 10: Lev 10-12, Matt 26:1-19
- ☐ Feb. 11: Lev 13, Matt 26:20-54
- ☐ Feb. 12: Lev 14, Matt 26:55-75
- ☐ Feb. 13: Lev 15-17, Matt 27:1-31
- ☐ Feb. 14: Lev 18-19, Matt 27:32-66
- ☐ Feb. 15: Lev 20-21, Matt 28:1-20
- ☐ Feb. 16: Lev 22-23, Mark 1:1-22
- ☐ Feb. 17: Lev 24-25, Mark 1:23-45
- ☐ Feb. 18: Lev 26-27, Mark 2
- ☐ Feb. 19: Num 1-2, Mark 3:1-21

☐ Feb. 20: Num 3-4, Mark 3:22-35
☐ Feb. 21: Num 5-6, Mark 4:1-20
☐ Feb. 22: Num 7, Mark 4:21-41
☐ Feb. 23: Num 8-10, Mark 5:1-20
☐ Feb. 24: Num 11-13, Mark 5:21-43
☐ Feb. 25: Num 14-15, Mark 6:1-32
☐ Feb. 26: Num 16-17, Mark 6:33-56
☐ Feb. 27: Num 18-20, Mark 7:1-13
☐ Feb. 28: Num 21-23, Mark 7:14-8:10

March

☐ Mar. 1: Num 24-27, Mark 8:11-38
☐ Mar. 2: Num 28-29, Mark 9:1-29
☐ Mar. 3: Num 30-31, Mark 9:30-50
☐ Mar. 4: Num 32-33, Mark 10:1-31
☐ Mar. 5: Num 34-36, Mark 10:32-52
☐ Mar. 6: Deut 1-2, Mark 11:1-19
☐ Mar. 7: Deut 3-4, Mark 11:20-33
☐ Mar. 8: Deut 5-7, Mark 12:1-27
☐ Mar. 9: Deut 8-10, Mark 12:28-44
☐ Mar. 10: Deut 11-13, Mark 13:1-13
☐ Mar. 11: Deut 14-16, Mark 13:14-37
☐ Mar. 12: Deut 17-19, Mark 14:1-25
☐ Mar. 13: Deut 20-22, Mark 14:26-50
☐ Mar. 14: Deut 23-25, Mark 14:51-72
☐ Mar. 15: Deut 26-27, Mark 15:1-26
☐ Mar. 16: Deut 28, Mark 15:27-47
☐ Mar. 17: Deut 29-30, Mark 16
☐ Mar. 18: Deut 31-32, Luke 1:1-23
☐ Mar. 19: Deut 33-34, Luke 1:24-56
☐ Mar. 20: Josh 1-3, Luke 1:57-80

- ☐ Mar. 21: Josh 4-6, Luke 2:1-24
- ☐ Mar. 22: Josh 7-8, Luke 2:25-52
- ☐ Mar. 23: Josh 9-10, Luke 3
- ☐ Mar. 24: Josh 11-13, Luke 4:1-32
- ☐ Mar. 25: Josh 14-15, Luke 4:33-44
- ☐ Mar. 26: Josh 16-18, Luke 5:1-16
- ☐ Mar. 27: Josh 19-20, Luke 5:17-39
- ☐ Mar. 28: Josh 21-22, Luke 6:1-26
- ☐ Mar. 29: Josh 23-24, Luke 6:27-49
- ☐ Mar. 30: Judg 1-2, Luke 7:1-30
- ☐ Mar. 31: Judg 3-5, Luke 7:31-50

April

- ☐ Apr. 1: Judg 6-7, Luke 8:1-21
- ☐ Apr. 2: Judg 8-9, Luke 8:22-56
- ☐ Apr. 3: Judg 10-11, Luke 9:1-36
- ☐ Apr. 4: Judg 12-14, Luke 9:37-62
- ☐ Apr. 5: Judg 15-17, Luke 10:1-24
- ☐ Apr. 6: Judg 18-19, Luke 10:25-42
- ☐ Apr. 7: Judg 20-21, Luke 11:1-28
- ☐ Apr. 8: Ruth 1-4, Luke 11:29-54
- ☐ Apr. 9: 1 Sam 1-3, Luke 12:1-34
- ☐ Apr. 10: 1 Sam 4-6, Luke 12:35-59
- ☐ Apr. 11: 1 Sam 7-9, Luke 13:1-21
- ☐ Apr. 12: 1 Sam 10-12, Luke 13:22-35
- ☐ Apr. 13: 1 Sam 13-14, Luke 14:12-24
- ☐ Apr. 14: 1 Sam 15-16, Luke 14:25-35
- ☐ Apr. 15: 1 Sam 17-18, Luke 15:1-10
- ☐ Apr. 16: 1 Sam 19-21, Luke 15:11-32
- ☐ Apr. 17: 1 Sam 22-24, Luke 16:1-18
- ☐ Apr. 18: 1 Sam 25-26, Luke 16:19-31

- ☐ Apr. 19: 1 Sam 27-29, Luke 17:1-19
- ☐ Apr. 20: 1 Sam 30-31, Luke 17:20-37
- ☐ Apr. 21: 2 Sam 1-3, Luke 18:1-17
- ☐ Apr. 22: 2 Sam 4-6, Luke 18:18-43
- ☐ Apr. 23: 2 Sam 7-9, Luke 19:1-28
- ☐ Apr. 24: 2 Sam 10-12, Luke 19:29-48
- ☐ Apr. 25: 2 Sam 13-14, Luke 20:1-26
- ☐ Apr. 26: 2 Sam 15-16, Luke 20:27-47
- ☐ Apr. 27: 2 Sam 17-18, Luke 21:1-19
- ☐ Apr. 28: 2 Sam 19-20, Luke 21:20-38
- ☐ Apr. 29: 2 Sam 21-22, Luke 22:1-30
- ☐ Apr. 30: 2 Sam 23-24, Luke 22:31-53

May

- ☐ May 1: 1 Kgs 1-2, Luke 22:54-71
- ☐ May 2: 1 Kgs 3-5, Luke 23:1-26
- ☐ May 3: 1 Kgs 6-7, Luke 23:27-38
- ☐ May 4: 1 Kgs 8-9, Luke 23:39-56
- ☐ May 5: 1 Kgs 10-11, Luke 24:1-35
- ☐ May 6: 1 Kgs 12-13, Luke 24:36-53
- ☐ May 7: 1 Kgs 14-15, John 1:1-28
- ☐ May 8: 1 Kgs 16-18, John 1:29-51
- ☐ May 9: 1 Kgs 19-20, John 2
- ☐ May 10: 1 Kgs 21-22, John 3:1-21
- ☐ May 11: 2 Kgs 1-3, John 3:22-36
- ☐ May 12: 2 Kgs 4-5, John 4:1-30
- ☐ May 13: 2 Kgs 6-8, John 4:31-54
- ☐ May 14: 2 Kgs 9-11, John 5:1-24
- ☐ May 15: 2 Kgs 12-14, John 5:25-47
- ☐ May 16: 2 Kgs 15-17, John 6:1-21
- ☐ May 17: 2 Kgs 18-19, John 6:22-44

- ☐ May 18: 2 Kgs 20-22, John 6:45-71
- ☐ May 19: 2 Kgs 23-25, John 7:1-31
- ☐ May 20: 1 Chr 1-2, John 7:32-53
- ☐ May 21: 1 Chr 3-5, John 8:1-20
- ☐ May 22: 1 Chr 6-7, John 8:21-36
- ☐ May 23: 1 Chr 8-10, John 8:37-59
- ☐ May 24: 1 Chr 11-13, John 9:1-23
- ☐ May 25: 1 Chr 14-16, John 9:24-41
- ☐ May 26: 1 Chr 17-19, John 10:1-21
- ☐ May 27: 1 Chr 20-22, John 10:22-42
- ☐ May 28: 1 Chr 23-25, John 11:1-17
- ☐ May 29: 1 Chr 26-27, John 11:18-46
- ☐ May 30: 1 Chr 28-29, John 11:47-57
- ☐ May 31: 2 Chr 1-3, John 12:1-19

June

- ☐ Jun 1: 2 Chr 4-6, John 12:20-50
- ☐ Jun 2: 2 Chr 7-9, John 13:1-17
- ☐ Jun 3: 2 Chr 10-12, John 13:18-38
- ☐ Jun 4: 2 Chr 13-16, John 14
- ☐ Jun 5: 2 Chr 17-19, John 15
- ☐ Jun 6: 2 Chr 20-22, John 16:1-15
- ☐ Jun 7: 2 Chr 23-25, John 16:16-33
- ☐ Jun 8: 2 Chr 26-28, John 17
- ☐ Jun 9: 2 Chr 29-31, John 18:1-23
- ☐ Jun 10: 2 Chr 32-33, John 18:24-40
- ☐ Jun 11: 2 Chr 34-36, John 19:1-22
- ☐ Jun 12: Ezra 1-2, John 19:23-42
- ☐ Jun 13: Ezra 3-5, John 20
- ☐ Jun 14: Ezra 6-8, John 21
- ☐ Jun 15: Ezra 9-10, Acts 1

☐ Jun 16: Neh 1-3, Acts 2:1-13
☐ Jun 17: Neh 4-6, Acts 2:14-47
☐ Jun 18: Neh 7-8, Acts 3
☐ Jun 19: Neh 9-11, Acts 4:1-22
☐ Jun 20: Neh 12-13, Acts 4:23-37
☐ Jun 21: Est 1-3, Acts 5:1-16
☐ Jun 22: Est 4-6, Acts 5:17-42
☐ Jun 23: Est 7-10, Acts 6
☐ Jun 24: Job 1-3, Acts 7:1-19
☐ Jun 25: Job 4-6, Acts 7:20-43
☐ Jun 26: Job 7-9, Acts 7:44-60
☐ Jun 27: Job 10-12, Acts 8:1-25
☐ Jun 28: Job 13-15, Acts 8:26-40
☐ Jun 29: Job 16-18, Acts 9:1-22
☐ Jun 30: Job 19-20, Acts 9:23-43

July

☐ Jul 1: Job 21-22, Acts 10:1-23
☐ Jul 2: Job 23-25, Acts 10:24-48
☐ Jul 3: Job 26-28, Acts 11
☐ Jul 4: Job 29-30, Acts 12
☐ Jul 5: Job 31-32, Acts 13:1-23
☐ Jul 6: Job 33-34, Acts 13:24-52
☐ Jul 7: Job 35-37, Acts 14
☐ Jul 8: Job 38-39, Acts 15:1-21
☐ Jul 9: Job 40-42, Acts 15:22-41
☐ Jul 10: Ps 1-3, Acts 16:1-15
☐ Jul 11: Ps 4-6, Acts 16:16-40
☐ Jul 12: Ps 7-9, Acts 17:1-15
☐ Jul 13: Ps 10-12, Acts 17:16-34
☐ Jul 14: Ps 13-16, Acts 18

- ☐ Jul 15: Ps 17-18, Acts 19:1-20
- ☐ Jul 16: Ps 19-21, Acts 19:21-41
- ☐ Jul 17: Ps 22-24, Acts 20:1-16
- ☐ Jul 18: Ps 25-27, Acts 20:17-38
- ☐ Jul 19: Ps 28-30, Acts 21:1-14
- ☐ Jul 20: Ps 31-33, Acts 21:15-40
- ☐ Jul 21: Ps 34-35, Acts 22
- ☐ Jul 22: Ps 36-37, Acts 23:1-11
- ☐ Jul 23: Ps 38-40, Acts 23:12-35
- ☐ Jul 24: Ps 41-43, Acts 24
- ☐ Jul 25: Ps 44-46, Acts 25
- ☐ Jul 26: Ps 47-49, Acts 26
- ☐ Jul 27: Ps 50-52, Acts 27:1-25
- ☐ Jul 28: Ps 53-55, Acts 27:26-44
- ☐ Jul 29: Ps 56-58, Acts 28:1-15
- ☐ Jul 30: Ps 59-61, Acts 28:16-31
- ☐ Jul 31: Ps 62-64, Rom 1

August

- ☐ Aug 1: Ps 65-67, Rom 2
- ☐ Aug 2: Ps 68-69, Rom 3
- ☐ Aug 3: Ps 70-72, Rom 4
- ☐ Aug 4: Ps 73-74, Rom 5
- ☐ Aug 5: Ps 75-77, Rom 6
- ☐ Aug 6: Ps 78, Rom 7
- ☐ Aug. 7: Ps 79-81, Rom 8:1-18
- ☐ Aug. 8: Ps 82-84, Rom 8:19-39
- ☐ Aug. 9: Ps 85-87, Rom 9
- ☐ Aug. 10: Ps 88-89, Rom 10
- ☐ Aug. 11: Ps 90-92, Rom 11:1-21
- ☐ Aug. 12: Ps 93-95, Rom 11:22-36

- ☐ Aug. 13: Ps 96-98, Rom 12
- ☐ Aug. 14: Ps 99-102, Rom 13
- ☐ Aug. 15: Ps 103-104, Rom 14
- ☐ Aug. 16: Ps 105-106, Rom 15:1-20
- ☐ Aug. 17: Ps 107-108, Rom 15:21-33
- ☐ Aug. 18: Ps 109-111, Rom 16
- ☐ Aug. 19: Ps 112-115, 1 Cor 1
- ☐ Aug. 20: Ps 116-118, 1 Cor 2
- ☐ Aug. 21: Ps 119:1-48, 1 Cor 3
- ☐ Aug. 22: Ps 119:49-104, 1 Cor 4
- ☐ Aug. 23: Ps 119:105-176, 1 Cor 5
- ☐ Aug. 24: Ps 120-123, 1 Cor 6
- ☐ Aug. 25: Ps 124-127, 1 Cor 7:1-24
- ☐ Aug. 26: Ps 128-131, 1 Cor 7:25-40
- ☐ Aug. 27: Ps 132-135, 1 Cor 8
- ☐ Aug. 28: Ps 136-138, 1 Cor 9
- ☐ Aug. 29: Ps 139-141, 1 Cor 10:1-13
- ☐ Aug. 30: Ps 142-144, 1 Cor 10:14-33
- ☐ Aug. 31: Ps 145-147, 1 Cor 11:1-15

September

- ☐ Sep. 1: Ps 148-150, 1 Cor 11:16-34
- ☐ Sep. 2: Prov 1-2, 1 Cor 12
- ☐ Sep. 3: Prov 3-4, 1 Cor 13
- ☐ Sep. 4: Prov 5-6, 1 Cor 14:1-20
- ☐ Sep. 5: Prov 7-8, 1 Cor 14:21-40
- ☐ Sep. 6: Prov 9-10, 1 Cor 15:1-32
- ☐ Sep. 7: Prov 11-12, 1 Cor 15:33-58
- ☐ Sep. 8: Prov 13-14, 1 Cor 16
- ☐ Sep. 9: Prov 15-16, 2 Cor 1
- ☐ Sep. 10: Prov 17-18, 2 Cor 2

- ☐ Sep. 11: Prov 19-20, 2 Cor 3
- ☐ Sep. 12: Prov 21-22, 2 Cor 4
- ☐ Sep. 13: Prov 23-24, 2 Cor 5
- ☐ Sep. 14: Prov 25-27, 2 Cor 6
- ☐ Sep. 15: Prov 28-29, 2 Cor 7
- ☐ Sep. 16: Prov 30-31, 2 Cor 8
- ☐ Sep. 17: Eccl 1-3, 2 Cor 9
- ☐ Sep. 18: Eccl 4-6, 2 Cor 10
- ☐ Sep. 19: Eccl 7-9, 2 Cor 11:1-15
- ☐ Sep. 20: Eccl 10-12, 2 Cor 11:16-33
- ☐ Sep. 21: Sng 1-3, 2 Cor 12
- ☐ Sep. 22: Sng 4-5, 2 Cor 13
- ☐ Sep. 23: Sng 6-8, Gal 1
- ☐ Sep. 24: Isa 1-3, Gal 2
- ☐ Sep. 25: Isa 4-6, Gal 3
- ☐ Sep. 26: Isa 7-9, Gal 4
- ☐ Sep. 27: Isa 10-12, Gal 5
- ☐ Sep. 28: Isa 13-15, Gal 6
- ☐ Sep. 29: Isa 16-18, Eph 1
- ☐ Sep. 30: Isa 19-21, Eph 2

October

- ☐ Oct. 1: Isa 22-23, Eph 3
- ☐ Oct. 2: Isa 24-26, Eph 4
- ☐ Oct. 3: Isa 27-28, Eph 5
- ☐ Oct. 4: Isa 29-30, Eph 6
- ☐ Oct. 5: Isa 31-33, Phil 1
- ☐ Oct. 6: Isa 34-36, Phil 2
- ☐ Oct. 7: Isa 37-38, Phil 3
- ☐ Oct. 8: Isa 39-40, Phil 4
- ☐ Oct. 9: Isa 41-42, Col 1

- ☐ Oct. 10: Isa 43-44, Col 2
- ☐ Oct. 11: Isa 45-47, Col 3
- ☐ Oct. 12: Isa 48-49, Col 4
- ☐ Oct. 13: Isa 50-52, 1 Thess 1
- ☐ Oct. 14: Isa 53-55, 1 Thess 2
- ☐ Oct. 15: Isa 56-58, 1 Thess 3
- ☐ Oct. 16: Isa 59-61, 1 Thess 4
- ☐ Oct. 17: Isa 62-64, 1 Thess 5
- ☐ Oct. 18: Isa 65-66, 2 Thess 1
- ☐ Oct. 19: Jer 1-2, 2 Thess 2
- ☐ Oct. 20: Jer 3-4, 2 Thess 3
- ☐ Oct. 21: Jer 5-6, 1 Tim 1
- ☐ Oct. 22: Jer 7-8, 1 Tim 2
- ☐ Oct. 23: Jer 9-10, 1 Tim 3
- ☐ Oct. 24: Jer 11-13, 1 Tim 4
- ☐ Oct. 25: Jer 14-16, 1 Tim 5
- ☐ Oct. 26: Jer 17-19, 1 Tim 6
- ☐ Oct. 27: Jer 20-22, 2 Tim 1
- ☐ Oct. 28: Jer 23-24, 2 Tim 2
- ☐ Oct. 29: Jer 25-26, 2 Tim 3
- ☐ Oct. 30: Jer 27-28, 2 Tim 4
- ☐ Oct. 31: Jer 29-30, Titus 1

November

- ☐ Nov. 1: Jer 31-32, Titus 2
- ☐ Nov. 2: Jer 33-35, Titus 3
- ☐ Nov. 3: Jer 36-37, Phm 1
- ☐ Nov. 4: Jer 38-39, Heb 1
- ☐ Nov. 5: Jer 40-42, Heb 2
- ☐ Nov. 6: Jer 43-45, Heb 3
- ☐ Nov. 7: Jer 46-48, Heb 4

- ☐ Nov. 8: Jer 49-50, Heb 5
- ☐ Nov. 9: Jer 51-52, Heb 6
- ☐ Nov. 10: Lam 1-2, Heb 7
- ☐ Nov. 11: Lam 3-5, Heb 8
- ☐ Nov. 12: Ezek 1-3, Heb 9
- ☐ Nov. 13: Ezek 4-6, Heb 10:1-23
- ☐ Nov. 14: Ezek 7-9, Heb 10:24-39
- ☐ Nov. 15: Ezek 10-12, Heb 11:1-19
- ☐ Nov. 16: Ezek 13-15, Heb 11:20-40
- ☐ Nov. 17: Ezek 16, Heb 12
- ☐ Nov. 18: Ezek 17-19, Heb 13
- ☐ Nov. 19: Ezek 20-21, Jas 1
- ☐ Nov. 20: Ezek 22-23, Jas 2
- ☐ Nov. 21: Ezek 24-26, Jas 3
- ☐ Nov. 22: Ezek 27-28, Jas 4
- ☐ Nov. 23: Ezek 29-31, Jas 5
- ☐ Nov. 24: Ezek 32-33, 1 Pet 1
- ☐ Nov. 25: Ezek 34-35, 1 Pet 2
- ☐ Nov. 26: Ezek 36-37, 1 Pet 3
- ☐ Nov. 27: Ezek 38-39, 1 Pet 4
- ☐ Nov. 28: Ezek 40, 1 Pet 5
- ☐ Nov. 29: Ezek 41-42, 2 Pet 1
- ☐ Nov. 30: Ezek 43-44, 2 Pet 2

December

- ☐ Dec. 1: Ezek 45-46, 2 Pet 3
- ☐ Dec. 2: Ezek 47-48, 1 John 1
- ☐ Dec. 3: Dan 1-2, 1 John 2
- ☐ Dec. 4: Dan 3-4, 1 John 3
- ☐ Dec. 5: Dan 5-6, 1 John 4
- ☐ Dec. 6: Dan 7-8, 1 John 5

- ☐ Dec. 7: Dan 9-10, 2 John 1
- ☐ Dec. 8: Dan 11-12, 3 John 1
- ☐ Dec. 9: Hos 1-4, Jude 1
- ☐ Dec. 10: Hos 5-8, Rev 1
- ☐ Dec. 11: Hos 9-11, Rev 2
- ☐ Dec. 12: Hos 12-14, Rev 3
- ☐ Dec. 13: Joel 1-3, Rev 4
- ☐ Dec. 14: Amos 1-3, Rev 5
- ☐ Dec. 15: Amos 4-6, Rev 6
- ☐ Dec. 16: Amos 7-9, Rev 7
- ☐ Dec. 17: Obad 1, Rev 8
- ☐ Dec. 18: Jonah 1-4, Rev 9
- ☐ Dec. 19: Mic 1-3, Rev 10
- ☐ Dec. 20: Mic 4-5, Rev 11
- ☐ Dec. 21: Mic 6-7, Rev 12
- ☐ Dec. 22: Nahum 1-3, Rev 13
- ☐ Dec. 23: Hab 1-3, Rev 14
- ☐ Dec. 24: Zeph 1-3, Rev 15
- ☐ Dec. 25: Hag 1-2, Rev 16
- ☐ Dec. 26: Zech 1-3, Rev 17
- ☐ Dec. 27: Zech 4-6, Rev 18
- ☐ Dec. 28: Zech 7-9, Rev 19
- ☐ Dec. 29: Zech 10-12, Rev 20
- ☐ Dec. 30: Zech 13-14, Rev 21
- ☐ Dec. 31: Mal 1-4, Rev 22

APPENDIX B

WHO I AM IN CHRIST
from Victory Over the Darkness by Neil T. Anderson, p. 38-39

I Am Accepted

- John 1:12 – I am God's child
- John 15:15 – I am Christ's friend
- Romans 5:1 – I have been justified
- 1 Corinthians 6:17 – I am united with the Lord, and I am one spirit with Him
- 1 Corinthians 6:20 – I have been bought with a price. I belong to God
- 1 Corinthians 12:27 – I am a member of Christ's body
- Ephesians 1:1 – I am a saint
- Ephesians 1:5 – I have been adopted as God's child
- Ephesians 2:18 – I have direct access to God through the Holy Spirit
- Colossians 1:14 – I have been redeemed and forgiven of all my sins
- Colossians 2:10 – I am complete in Christ
- 1 Thessalonians 5:9 – I am destined to be saved by Jesus Christ, who died for me
- I am the salt of the earth (Matt. 5:13)
- I am the light of the world (Matt. 5:14)
- I am a child of God (John 1:12 & Rom 8:16)

- I am part of the true vine, a channel of Christ's life (John 15:1, 5)
- I am Christ's friend (John 15:15)
- I am chosen and appointed by Christ to bear fruit (John 15:16)
- I am a slave of righteousness (Rom. 6:18)
- I am enslaved to God (Rom. 6:22)
- I am a son of God; God is spiritually my Father (Rom. 8:14, 15; Gal. 3:26; 4:6)
- I am a temple—a dwelling place—of God. His Spirit and His life dwell in me (1 Cor. 3:16; 6:19)
- I am united to the Lord and am one spirit with Him (1 Cor. 6:17)
- I am a member of Christ's Body (1 Cor. 12:27; Eph. 5:30)
- I am a new creation (2 Cor. 5:17)
- I am reconciled to God and am a minister of reconciliation (2 Cor. 5:18, 19)
- I am a son of God and one in Christ (Gal. 3:26, 28)
- I am an heir of God since I am a son of God (Gal. 4:6, 7)
- I am a saint (1 Cor. 1:2; Eph. 1:1; Phil. 1:1; Col. 1:2)

I Am Secure

- Romans 8:1-2 – I am free from condemnation
- Romans 8:28 – I am assured that all things work together for good
- Romans 8:31-34 – I am free from any condemning charges against me
- Romans 8:35-39 – I cannot be separated from the love of God
- 2 Corinthians 1:21-22 – I have been established, anointed and sealed by God

- Philippians 1:6 – I am confident that the good work God has begun in me will be perfected
- Philippians 3:20 – I am a citizen of heaven
- Colossians 3:3 – I am hidden with Christ in God
- 2 Timothy 1:7 – I have not been given a spirit of fear, but of power, love and a sound mind
- Hebrews 4:16 – I can find grace and mercy in time of need
- 1 John 5:18 – I am born of God and the evil one cannot touch me
- I am God's workmanship—His handiwork—born anew in Christ to do His work (Eph. 2:10)
- I am a fellow citizen with the rest of God's family (Eph. 2:19)
- I am a prisoner of Christ (Eph. 3:1; 4:1)
- I am righteous and holy (Eph. 4:24)
- I am a citizen of heaven, seated in heaven right now (Eph. 2:6; Phil. 3:20)
- I am hidden with Christ in God (Col. 3:3)
- I am an expression of the life of Christ because He is my life (Col. 3:4)
- I am chosen of God, holy and dearly loved (Col. 3:12; 1 Thess. 1:4)
- I am a son of light and not of darkness (1 Thess. 5:5)
- I am a holy partaker of a heavenly calling (Heb. 3:1)
- I am a partaker of Christ; I share in His life (Heb. 3:14)
- I am one of God's living stones, 'being built up in Christ as a spiritual house (1 Pet. 2:5)
- I am a member of a chosen race, a royal priesthood, a holy nation, a people of God's own possession (1 Pet. 2:9, 10)

- I am an alien and a stranger to this world in which I temporarily live (1 Pet. 2:11)

I Am Significant

- Matthew 5:13-14 – I am the salt and light of the earth
- John 15:1 & 5 – I am a branch of the true vine, a channel of His life
- John 15:16 – I have been chosen and appointed to bear fruit
- Acts 1:8 – I am a personal witness of Christ
- 1 Corinthians 3:16 – I am God's temple
- 2 Corinthians 5:17-21 – I am a minister [an ambassador] of reconciliation for God
- 2 Corinthians 6:1 – I am God's coworker (see 1 Cor. 3:9)
- Ephesians 2:6 – I am seated with Christ in the heavenly realm
- Ephesians 2:10 – I am God's workmanship
- Ephesians 3:12 – I may approach God with freedom and confidence
- Philippians 4:13 – I can do all things through Christ who strengthens me
- I am an enemy of the devil (1 Pet. 5:8)
- I am a child of God and I will resemble Christ when He returns (1 John 3:1, 2; Phil. 3:21)
- I am born of God, and the evil one—the devil—cannot touch me (1 John 5:18)
- I am not the great "I AM" (Ex. 3:14; John 8:24, 28, 58), but by the grace of God, I am what I am and God's grace toward me is not in vain (1 Cor. 15:10)

APPENDIX C – RESOURCES

TO HELP YOU GROW AS A CHRISTIAN

Neil T. Anderson

- *Victory Over the Darkness: Realizing the Power of Your Identity in Christ.* Ventura, CA: Regal Books, 2000.

Mark T. Barclay – www.marktbarclay.com

- *Avoiding the Pitfalls of Familiarity.* Midland, MI: Mark Barclay Publications, 1989.
- *How to Relate to Your Pastor.* Midland, MI: Mark Barclay Publications, 1995.
- *The Real Truth About Tithing.* Midland, MI: Mark Barclay Publications, 1994.

Kenny Gatlin – www.kennygatlinministries.com

- *How You Can Be Fruitful, Stable and Completely Immovable.* Midland, MI: Mark Barclay Publications, 2006.

E. W. Kenyon

- *The Bible in the Light of Our Redemption,* 28th Printing. Lynnwood, WA: Kenyon's Gospel Publishing Society, 2011.

Robert Morris

- *The Power of Your Words: How God Can Bless Your Life Through the Words You Speak.* Bloomington, MN: Bethany House Publishers, 2006.

Walt Straughan – www.wsmin.org

- *By Jesus' 39 Stripes We Were Healed.* Staunton, VA: Walt Straughan Ministries, 1990.

www.ingramcontent.com/pod-product-compliance
Lightning Source LLC
Chambersburg PA
CBHW071713040426
42446CB00011B/2052